Conquering Animal
MYSTICISM

Other books by this author

When Grandmother Speaks
Where Did My Dog Go?

Conquering Animal MYSTICISM

The Angelic Roles of Your Pet—
Stories of Sacred Messages
Communicated to Guardians

Donna Sauer, PhD

Copyright © Donna Sauer, PhD

All rights reserved. No part of this manuscript may be reproduced (by any means) or utilized in any form, electronic or mechanical.

ISBN (paperback): 979-8-218-08554-4
ISBN (ebook): 979-8-218-12926-2

Cover Image: istock
Cover and Interior design:
Christy Day, Constellation Book Services

Printed in the United States of America

DEDICATIONS

My profound gratefulness goes to—

> all the animals and their human guardians who contributed so lovingly to this book,
> my intrepid proofreader, Michael. I could not have done this without you,
> friends Tina and Linda for non-stop encouragement and needed refreshment of spirit,
> my guides and angels who knew my spiritual intent for this book and "made it so,"
> Psychic Sterling for his contribution to the title of this book,
> and my present beloved family of animals who patiently adored me even when the hours dedicated to completion of the book droned on and on.

Contents

Preface — *ix*

INTRODUCTION — 1

CHAPTER 1 — 3
Recognizing the Animals as Pure Spirits Connected to the Divine Source

CHAPTER 2 — 9
Love is Joy Untethered—Experiencing the Communal Vibrations Between Animals and Humans

CHAPTER 3 — 21
Living in the Moment

CHAPTER 4 — 31
Sacred Soul Contracts—The Divine Purposes of Animals

CHAPTER 5 — 53
Animals As Protectors, Healers, Sources of Laughter and Bliss

CHAPTER 6 — 69
Spiritual Guidance Through the Teachings of the Animals

CHAPTER 7 — 77
TRUST AND LOSS A Lesson of Experiencing Animal Mysticism Through the Loss of a Beloved Pet

CHAPTER 8 93
GROWING OLD — Eternal Love, Lingering Memories,
Stories of Forever Bonds

CHAPTER 9 105
The Little Ones 105

CHAPTER 10 115
Conquering Animal Mysticism—The Final Illumination

References *122*

PREFACE

Readers may wonder how and why an author came to write a book. As an Animal Communicator and Energy Healer I have often thought how wonderful it would be if any person could simply hear the animals' messages just as they are spoken to me. How exciting for any human not only to experience bonding with the physical manifestation of animals and to understand their wants and needs, their illnesses, their happiest moments, their personalities (which are as diverse as any group of humans), but also to embrace the spiritual side of animals, their high angelic vibrational energies, by which they bring messages of unconditional love and healing.

In meditation, asking for guidance to write this book, I received this spiritual message from the animals who were shown in a semi-circle of animals around me:

"You are one of us. We stand in your stead. One by one we step forward. We extend our helping hand, our love and support. Do not be discouraged. Your book will be completed and circulated to bring hope and it will be cherished by many.

Your goal is to help others recognize the ALL, the Universal Oneness, the Source, the Lakota Wankan' Tanka (the Sacred Greatness) in animals and to be receptive to their loving messages. You must do this on your own—no hints, no earthly support. Bring in your higher self and be creative and bold. Laugh with your own little ones and absorb their love as you write."

I was then shown first my whole office suffused with purple haze as my living pets were sleeping at my feet, and then a large purple candle flamed up and from it a thousand tiny lit candles in the dark spread out over a large flat plain. I was told these were "all my animals."

"All my animals" then said to me:

"Do not let our sacrifices and loves and stories and messages be forgotten. Do not let our spirits fade into nothingness with no one remembering and learning from our lives. You must get our stories written down. Our stories need to go out to the millions to soothe, to give hope, to teach how to believe in the infinite love of the ALL. You alone can tell our stories of the sacred compassion and caring which is within every being. Do not let us down. Be strong and productive. You well know Mitakuye Oyasin—'All my relations.' Move on, our dear daughter. Your path is clear—and cleared for you. We manifest those to edit and publish this book. Bring love, think love, be love. That is all there is to living, dear one."

Thus my book, *Conquering Animal Mysticism*, was written. Wherever it is picked up and read, readers will be receiving the wonder and excitement of knowing their very own pets are creatures of great spirituality. *Conquering Animal Mysticism* will become part of their hearts in whole and in love.

INTRODUCTION

What is MYSTICISM? Mysticism is the channeling of information of the ultimate or hidden higher truths, given to the messengers, the mystics, from the Universal Being, the All, the One Source, Creator, the Great Unknown. It is becoming one with or having union with the Spirit of Unconditional Absolute Love, the Infinite, the Great Mystery. Attainment of insight into these truths of the all-loving spirit brings a release to be in the present, allowing the transfer of divine truth and acceptance. The result is the harmony Creator instilled in each of us because all cosmic truths are applied to create harmony among souls. Thus cometh our sacred animals, the angels of mysticism, carrying their messages from Creator to us.

Art is creating what is unknown about us. The Great Unknown is, of course, around and within each of us, but when the creative art of an animal communicator and energy healer is used, the expansion of understanding comes through from the beloved animal mystics. The glowing of shared love is palpable. There is no more thorough unfolding of the Universal Oneness than communicating with the animals wherein a miracle occurs, a sharing of higher angelic frequency vibrations.

Who knew animals could talk? Of course, they can. It is the listener who is deficient if the words be not heard. With more than words comes the compassion and individuality of each animal. They shine with their own grace, teachings, and healings of energy for their guardians. They have, of course, their own divine purposes in their physical lives, but they choose to come to help bring us to our higher selves, to support us in our chosen pathways, to elevate our souls with life lessons.

The messages they bring are of joyful happiness, of contemplation and of being in the moment, of learning to grieve a loss while being given strength and wisdom for having had that loss, and of experiencing love in the warming light of total non-judgement and acceptance from another being.

This book is all about illumination through stories of animal mysticism. Your life path has brought you to this book for comfort and direction concerning the animals. Whether they are still on this plane or crossed over, all who have touched you with their presence and energy bring you understanding of absolute and nonjudgemental love through their magnificent mysticism.

CHAPTER 1

Recognizing the Animals as Pure Spirits Connected to the Divine Source

Connecting to the Divine Source (Creator, Great Unknown, God) shows one an absolute love in a bright and clear picture, a pathway, a message. That image, that knowing, implies trust in this expanding unconditional, nonjudgemental love that brings the highest good and wellbeing for each and all.

Our connection to Divine Source is always through the magical energy of vibrational frequency. To understand the spirituality of your animal companion, it is necessary to begin with this very concept: as with people, every animal and living thing is unique. The essence of each animal is an entity with a unique singular vibrational frequency that exists for all times in all dimensions. It is this that is the soul of each human and animal, the pure energy of sacred unconditional love.

A soul, is pure energy and as such, can never be created or destroyed. It exists whether housed as a spirit in a physical body on earth or wholly in the spiritual world after crossing over. What we experience with our senses in the physical plane can be described as an illusion in that objects and soul-beings are not really separate, time is not linear but fluid and flowing, and there is no distance between us and others, all who have passed and who are yet to be born. We are at once one and everywhere. In a way, each of us creates our own physical, emotional, and spiritual reality in our living existence on earth, using our spirit's intentional plan for harmony and peace.

The quest of living in the physical state on earth is having experiences that create love, sustain love, and create the vibrations of love. Such vibrations are truly eternal and never cease to exist in the universe, in all dimensions, in all times. Animals do this so beautifully and it is of no surprise they carry this mysticism of energy and love when they cross over to become a seraphic being.

Communications with those who have crossed over bring messages through the human reader acting as a conduit (the "hollow bone" in some Native American traditions). Much healing and calming and happiness for grieving guardians is possible, bringing salve and consolation through their sacred lessons and stories.

Animals do exist at once both as a physical and as a spiritual being. Some may even have chosen to reincarnate in an animal body to rejoin an earthly family. Whatever the sharing, the animal must be honored by us and shown how grateful we are for them being in our life. Acknowledge them, talk to them, laugh and play with them.

Care for them in non-judgmental and total accepting ways. Love them and give them the courtesy one would to any human member of the family. Explain to them in everyday life why we are leaving the house and when we will return. Send them mind pictures while apart, showing them where we are and what we are doing. Ask them what they need and how we can make their life the best it can be. Ask them to sit with us in relaxation and meditation. Learn to be in the moment with them.

All animals are part of the angelic realm. They are a legion of angels, pure spirits, connected directly to the Divine Love. Their elevated vibrational frequencies in the spiritual plane are of very high energy, on par with that of the angels. Existing as they do in the spiritual plane, they can choose to come back to the physical plane on earth, acting as mystics, bringing messages and unconditional love. They come as a gift to humans, always acting as teachers and healers—"angels on earth" if you like. They are elevated entities who can indeed communicate with their humans on the same channels as angels and guides. They can also easily communicate psychically with the vibrational frequencies of other animals, plants and crossed-over beings.

This higher order of mysticism is meant to bring guardians of pets an awareness of both why the animal came to be with them and how the animal has chosen to help their humans grow in their spiritual life path. Animals choose the family in which they will live and for how long they will remain as part of a contract between that family and the animal, created long before the animal was born into its physical being. A guardian acknowledging that sacred bond, and grasping on to it during shared physical lifetimes, brings them both elevated states of love, energy, and sharing.

Animals, as spiritual beings, choose when and where and how and why and for how long they will transition into a physical body. In that context, your pet chooses you to be its companion. Much of this interconnection comes as a spiritual contract, that is a divine mission or blueprint, which is a process begun and decided upon before either the guardian or the pet has returned to earthly form. In these spiritual contracts, each animal and person who may come in contact during this lifetime, create the spiritual pathway between them. It is a blueprint which determines how they will interact, what lessons will be learned, how long of a time they will share, and so forth. The contact between animal and human may be quite short or very long. It may be a deep bond of love with a good, loyal funny dog or a more light companionship or even a brief encounter such as having a butterfly sit on your hand or accidentally running over a turtle on the road. A pet will go to great lengths to "set up" the steps necessary to fulfill this divine contract. They come specifically to help us as well as complete their own life path of experiences.

Importantly, the spiritual interaction does not end with a pet's death or a guardian's death but continues as a constant connection between them which is ever-lasting love and devotion. A companion animal is able to remain in spirit around their human companions after crossing over, continuing to comfort, heal, and help with learning of life lessons. Animals in spirit may have lived with many families during their lifetime and can travel freely, being at once with multiple people and other animals. Asking them to be around you for comfort and support is not taxing. They can be with everyone and everywhere at once. Time is not limiting to them.

Communicating, connecting, doing healing work as an Animal Communicator and Energy Healer thus is always for all dimensions and for all times. Being in psychic communion with animal-being vibrational frequencies can be done in the presence of living animal as easily as over a long geographical distance and as well with any animal existing in the spiritual realm after crossing over.

Any human can connect to this angelic light of creatures through the pulsating energy (frequency) by which spiritual messages of love and compassion are transmitted and expressed, messages full of understanding, love, and total acceptance, Discovering the ability of psychic communication with the animals is an exhilarating experience. Perception of self seems to unfold like the petals of a flower, expanding our very being into the universe. In this sense, the animals became our axis mundi, the angelic connection between heaven and earth.

Thus the seraphic self of an animal comes as a gift to earth and to specific people, acting always as a wise and compassionate teacher and healer. Each brings the Universal Consciousness to humans by bonding and teaching unconditional judgement. Be grateful for the animals. Honor their commitment and sacrifice by expressing gratitude, giving thanks for their lessons and gifts, and interacting with them in ways that are for their highest good, physically, emotionally, spiritually. Their mysticism brings us great love directly from the Divine Universal Source, helping us choose pure living intention in the path of high vibrational frequency growth for our souls, teaching absolute acceptance without caveats in our giving to others.

With that spreading of light and healing in mind, this book brings stories of love, repair, hope, and understanding from the animals themselves. And, possibly, the love and sharing intentioned and manifested by each and every animal with which we have had communal pathways, will bring illumination and gratefulness of the mysticism of these, our very own angelic beings.

Conquering Animal Mysticism

CHAPTER 2

Love is Joy Untethered—
Experiencing the Communal Vibrations
Between Animals and Humans

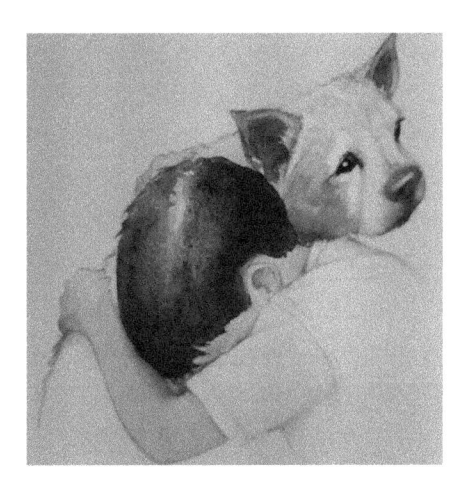

To understand the mysticism of animals, we must accept the concept of connection between animals and humans in a new shimmering exciting way. There is a shared relationship for all beings and all things in the communal frequencies of vibration of energy, from the smallest molecules to the greatest mountains, from the tiniest of spiders to the ancient redwoods, from ourselves to everything.

But connection is really also a spiritual continuum from the present back to past lives and the Ancestors and the Star Nations and forward to the future, not really in a linear timeline but rather as a vast confluence of all things in all times, in all planes, known and unknown. Einstein presented us with the idea that "all time is occurring at once." Everything is a part of the now as we can touch the past and future simultaneously. We as mortals get a glimpse of this important truth when we experience memories of an animal from the past, when we accept that a soul and its spirit-truths of love exist forever. Then we settle into understanding that we have created our lives in a shared sacred path with a past pet that richly gave lessons and experiences needed for our spiritual growth.

Connecting to the Great Unknown through mysticism words of an animal show us what might be called "grace" or "the universal truths." The importance is in our trust that there is a purposeful spreading of that grace in all times and dimensions for the greatest good of all. To accept connection is to embrace the marvelous idea that all animals are beings of pure energy which exist without end. It means taking that single brave leap over that canyon of doubt and you now embrace animals as fellow souls, acknowledging they are elevated spirits on earth, part of the angelic realm who come into physical body purely to help us learn lessons, share their healing, bring companionship and joy.

Energy frequencies come to match in animal psychic work. Generally speaking, animals coming from the angelic realm of high frequency energies have to lower their vibrations, to "come down" to the human level which they can do quite easily. They come always in a sense of white light and protection. Conversely, each of us needs to be in a quiet sense of light and love wherein we can raise our own vibrational energy to meet with them, to be near them, to feel their energy, to have a conversation with them.

It is a wonderful way to learn to communicate. Never wonder

that animals can read our thoughts and each other easily. They wish us to go in peace, to create and share love and, importantly, laughter. They are our connection to paradise, so to speak.

As an Animal Communicator, my connection always begins by asking permission of the animal which may be as simple as just bringing them to mind or heart or formally making a request. The connection request is an honoring of their unique being and seeks them out to "come in" to me, to be near me, to share their energy so we can have a conversation.

Any pet comes to my animal communication readings in two ways. One is as the dog or cat or horse level of just being the animal they came to experience in this lifetime. They describe fun toys, good food, happy hikes, sorrow at losing a member of the family, their medical ailments, anxiety at being left alone. The other is more spiritual. In my experiences, pets will then leave this level of connection and move on to a second level in which they express spiritual matters they want to send to their guardians. These may be an expression of joy at watching their guardian growing vibrations of love in their chosen life path, or perhaps urging their human companion to branch into new creative work, or asking them to expand psychic abilities to help others.

PHILLIP

Here then is a lovely illustrative session with a Pineapple Conure. He is 4 years old and lives with a guardian who is herself an intuitive healer.

(Please note that all conversations I scribed directly from the animals are in bold print.)

First, though, before our session began, came an endearing spontaneous download from Phillip as I was thinking of starting his reading and wondering how he came to be, what experiences he had had already.

Phillip's Message
May 19, 2021

"Well, you know—you are out in the ether, hovering, waiting. Then the egg and sperm connect. The protein molecules coalesce.

Zip, Zoom, Bam—cells multiply, then a thin membrane and then a thicker shell.

Whoa!—watching, watching—wait for it. Egg laid in the nest. Looking good.

Still warm and comfy—still dark. Mum above me and I feel her energy.

Every now and then, the egg gets rolled. OK—my tummy is up to this. Head and neck still curved over my belly. Way huge sac of fat there—I am growing, growing.

Oh, Oh—getting cramped. Hey, I can talk—and my Mum is cooing back. Feeling the urge to start pounding the old beak on the wall. Crack-crack. Holy cow—a chip falls off—light at last.

Full from spirit into my body now—healthy body, ready to rock and roll.

Yep—pop right out of that hard shell. Fluff drying the old wet feathers. Feeling the warm dry feathers of Mum above me, enclosing me. All is safe.

Soon enough —time to start chirping for food. This is a cup of tea! Food on demand. Good deal.

Feeling strong—really liking the light. Vibrating with energy. Thinking in the spiritual of the path ahead—all laid out. But for now—one breath at a time, one cheep, one meal—and soon, one step.

And then, oh then, flight—freedom, soaring, hopping branches, full and safe in the bright sun.

And THAT is how I was born, dear Ma."

This was followed by the communication I had with Phillip during his full energy balancing session.

Phillip, may I have your permission to do this reading with you today?

PHILLIP. "Sure, Ma. Me own Mum will be here with us, of course. She is getting much better at 'reading' all of us animals but we are nudging, baby steps, into accepting and growing this 'angle' of her intuitive work. You can observe for yourself her stronger self-assuredness in all of this work. We prefer not to call this 'work' because in the spiritual sense, it is a vibrational elevation that is joy and gratitude and guiding, so many others to see their inner oneness with the All. So perhaps a better term or description would be 'polishing the sheen of the loving energy' that is within and without everyone and everything.

Can you please tell her these words? I am the spokesman today for all the animals around her. These are also their words and their wishes and love for her. The circle of us all makes her enlightenment and opening more exuberant and gay and very shared as her art work and her interactions occur.

As an aside, please tell my Mum that it is me who suggests—strongly I might add— that she add her green colors. It gives me much pleasure to conjure (haha—get the play on words here) up my ancestral and ancient roots in tropical greens of all shades and hues. I am filled with contentment and joy when this happens—and whenever I am free in the physical to hop around the branches and leaves of greenery."

May I speak further with you at this time, Phillip?

PHILLIP. "Sure, Ma. But I think I conveyed all the good stuff I wanted to say. My Mum intuits most of my feelings and needs herself. Just to please let her know how happy and grateful I am to be in this house, this family, this energy emanating from my Mum. If there could be a description understandable to humans, I would call this life of mine 'heaven on earth.' Ecstatic happiness and unconditional acceptance of me just as I am. I send the same back to every being around me, but Mum can feel my love best. She absorbs it and feels the 'happy' from me."

Anything else, Phillip?

PHILLIP. "No, Ma. Go in peace."

Animals in their communications bring messages and guidance for humans which bring the comfort of releasing guilt or sorrow for the manner or time of crossing-over. Animals express their gratefulness for their care and love. Moving into higher spiritual matters, they will describe how the guardian's own soul has grown and developed because of their shared life paths (their divine contract purposes) and encourages them to continue in their life pathway to higher creative blossoming and love. The pet will explain how it will guide and support their guardian, opening up new vistas in their "light work" of the Universal All.

Connecting with a pet or any animal who has crossed over into spirit form is quite easily done. Animals that cross over are instantly in the energy of divine love with total awareness and acceptance. They immediately are able to communicate, showing validations with remembrance of moments of laughter, of illness and pain, of joy. And they will give information on past lives that they have shared with their guardian and whether they will reincarnate, possibly into the guardian's present lifetime. They may explain how and when a new pet is being guided to their guardian by color, age, adoption, name, sex, age—or even what type of animal. Always stressed to the guardian is the non-judgmental acceptance and total love of the new animal as its own persona. They will guide the new pet in adapting to living with the guardian, making the bonding and behavior smoother and of a higher order.

GRIZZ

The following story is of a psychic-medium session in which a crossed over dog named Grizz expounded on his spiritual connections with his "Mum" Charlene. He is most certainly an elevated soul and is very eager for her to continue in her own psychic "light work" wherein he will be with her as always. And too he gently helps to relieve her of the burden of guilt she had for his passing, allowing her to move forward in love and not sorrow.

Grizz was a male husky, wolf, heeler mix who crossed over at 13 years of age five weeks previous to my session with him. His guardian, Charlene, asked if he was happy, where he is, if he has forgiven her for not going back with him to the room where he was put to sleep, if he is upset she has not yet gone to visit his grave, and that she wanted him to know he was the best dog and gave her 13 years of joy.

GRIZZ'S MESSAGE
November 1, 2019

Grizz, may I speak with you at this time?

GRIZZ. "Sure, Ma. This is such a happy coincidence as I was just sending my Mum loving, healing messages and I DO think she is 'getting it,' that is, I am with her as I ever was. She is coming into that understanding and acceptance of the wider energies we share, of the expanding loves we have now that I am in spiritual. My Mum is moving into this expanse, this knowing. I am bursting with joy as she learns, grows (and growls beautifully) with me as ever we did totally in the physical. I dance with joy. *(I saw him on his back legs, twirling, exuberant).* This is it—this is the moment, this is the time. Her heart beats with the happy rhythm of bongo beats and music of the stars as she joins me in this dance of the Ancestors and the Star Nation. She needs to live it, feel it, move forward in the ecstasy of living for the spirit of herself and for the energies, blessed energies of all around her. There is a particular large tree near her which she needs to hug, to stroke, to send gratitude to for the many times of consoling and bearing her up and bringing in the strength she needed at that time. Do not let this 'old one' go unthanked."

(The guardian, Charlene, acknowledged the presence of such a tree at her home and the loving strong connection they shared.)

He started to walk sedately towards me through a tunnel of white love and light between our hearts and then suddenly put on a burst of speed and skidded to a stop in front of me. Sitting down, he looked up and said:

"See, Ma. What beautiful, powerful energy and strength I have now. I feel so expansive, so ready to 'work' for the love and growth that honors the All. Please tell my Mum about this beauty and fluidity I have now and how happy I am to be here, joining in the efforts, the pushing, the blowing forward and outward, of all the love and good deeds and compassion everywhere and everyone getting accomplished. I am so 'ALIVE' with this work, so energetic.

I do so much want my Mum to join in this work. There is much to be done, as she is so very aware. Not to be afraid, Mum, as I am with you every step, every leap, every song and laughter along the way of the future.

Please let my Mum know I am aware and feel her sorrow at my passing and not having my physical warm body near her. This will pass, my dear Mum, as you realize and grow into the bigger knowing that my spirit, my energy, my being, my vibration of existence that once was enclosed in a furry wolfie body is as it ever was—full of love and compassion, coming close to you, Mum.

Please ask her not to visit my grave for a while. I am not there of course, but when she feels ready, I will walk by her side as she approaches that place. She need only put her hand down beside her as she walks and feel my energy beside her. Ask her to bring with her a photo, a candle, and a piece of my favorite candy. Light the candle, thank me for sharing our life together, send gratitude to me for a life well-lived, and spend some moments remembering me at my most healthy, exuberant, happy, giddy self, for that is just as I am now. By recognizing my being in spirit and taking on my spirit being in total as being with her, she will leave that grave site in beautiful spirit, in happy relief, in a joyful heart, knowing that nothing has diminished for me or for her or for what is still being exchanged in love and happiness between us at all times.

Please tell me Mum there is to be no guilt at not accompanying me to the room where I was euthanized. I was already moving my spirit to prepare for crossing and her great grief being present with me might have pulled me back, making my crossing less easy. I was ready to cross, had all 'my ducks in a row,' so to speak. I chose the crossing experience I wanted for my own self and we agreed in our 'soul contract' before returning to the physical world this last time that you would allow me that experience of crossing alone without you near. And you also agreed to experience that great grief and aloneness as I left the room to pass out of my physical body. All is as we planned it, all went just as we agreed long ago. All is good and beautiful and fulfilled. Please tell her to remember our eternal connection in her soul self, from that long time ago, and she will be comforted.

I am with my Mum at all times. Ask her to take deep breaths, be calm, bring in good energy, and feel my breath on her face. There will be a whiff of white cloud around her at times as I bring the smoke of the Ancient Ones' campfires to her to purify and soothe. Her ancestors welcome her to the hearth, to the connected sharing of all that ever was and all that is and all that will ever be.

Go in peace, Ma."

CHAPTER 3

Living in the Moment

To live in the moment is perhaps the greatest gift our animals teach us. To be totally "alive" for them is to breathe in the rain and the sun equally, to love just being. Animals do not harbor regrets for the past or concern themselves with what might happen a week from now.

They are free.

Yes, animals living as physical beings may have lingering physical or emotional damage from abuse or abandonment by humans, or may mourn the loss of a companion as might any living creature, and there are stories of life long devotion waiting for their human companion to return. But given time and love to heal, they generally again become the sunny trusting personality of a physical self needing to be happy, content, and sharing love.

In animal communication sessions I reach that traumatized or grieving animal and help them better understand at the physical and emotional level how they might heal. But their higher seraphic selves are well aware of all that is unfolding. Their sacrifice of well being or even of their life is a gift, a lesson for the human around them. It is implicit on people to realize that every injury or mistreatment or angry word or willful ignorance an animal suffers is a lesson offered, a chance for the human to grow in grace and love.

Being cruel is a very low energy state, one that our animals urge us to leave behind and learn to love and live in the precious moment of life given. Every empathetic help and care for an injured, frightened, needing animal elevates a human to that higher vibration which adds to the love of the universe, a way of being in the moment with the greatest love.

There is nothing more unfolding of the Great Unknown to me than doing the readings of my work in Animal Energy Healing and Communication. Each reading is a minor miracle, a sharing of higher loving frequency vibrations with animals and plants. I am given new lessons each and every time, my way of being in the moment to help others, the glowing of shared love when I am in the vibrational synchrony with an animal soul. And always comes my gratitude to the animal for sharing and allowing me to be with them.

Many animal communication readings exemplify the ability of animals to be sweetly present and to amplify the importance for us of being in the moment. Whatever has happened in the past, you have the option to leave it behind you, live in the moment, and be happy. That is what animals do and that is what they teach us.

ANGEL

This is a story of a small white dog who lived bigly in the moment, even in the discomfort of old age ailments. She was a beautiful glowing being of light who taught me every day the finesse of acceptance, calmness, and absorption of the healing nature around me and how to give love and care unending to a small creature whose name apropos was Angel.

Angel was of unknown ancestry and was gifted to me by a family after the elderly mother and father both died within a few months. She readily moved into our extended family of dogs and cats in a country home as if she had always been there. Quiet and happy, she was one of the gang.

As she aged over the years, she became a bit stiff and in the last years was incontinent, always suffering the indignity of diaper changes without protest. Her most favorite ritual was to lay in the sun, front paws crossed over one another, head up inhaling the scents on the breeze. At those times, she seemed one with the earth, a contentment which I have found hard at times to embrace as a lesson from her. She was as "in the moment" as any creature could ever be. After Angel's death, she continues to be with me. The other animals sense her bouncy presence and she appears as a floating orb under the apple tree when I sit outside of a summer afternoon. She is in death as alive and bright as ever and makes me smile. I am forever grateful to have shared her life.

Angel's Message
December 10, 2016

"**In old age with many infirmities, I chose always to be in tune with the 'now' and practiced that with intensity, that is, to be very much aware of being present. My needs were not complex and I had come to experience life in the moment, always knowing the past is the past. Colors, odors, touch, sounds—levels and layers—all gave me enjoyment and in a spiritual sense, I was within the orchestration of what was right now. I was not just having a simple life in a** doggie body but rather a fully contemplative and experiential living.

I asked after I died in July for a 'proper moon ceremony' to honor me. My mother carried that out for me with the Lakota prayers and songs she lovingly sent and I am grateful and my heart is full of love for her caring."

(July is the Lakota Canpasapa Wi, the moon when the choke cherries are ripe. It is a time of healing, remembrance of those who have crossed-over, and renewal, celebrated in the traditional Sundance. In Lakota ways, the Big Dipper's 7 stars (which are related to the 7 council fires, the 7 stages of womanhood, etc) ferry the spiritual essence of the deceased ones to the Milky Way, called the Trail of the Spirits or the Way of the Souls,. This is the trail all Lakota take after death. Those who lived a "proper" life take the road to the promised land of departed souls—that Star Nation, the ancestors—where they are always honored in prayers and ceremonies. So when my sweet Angel asked for a "proper moon" Lakota ceremony, she was encompassing so much, so many layers of spirituality. I was honored to be able to do that for her.)

"I sensed the rhythmic ebb and flow
in the breath of the world
and practiced that breathing
with the intensity of the living in the moment
of All that is."

TONI JO

Toni Jo is an elderly black Labrador Retriever. She is an old soul, experiencing many lifetimes, always with the intent of healing and teaching and guiding. Her many wise lessons come through to enlighten and uplift, smoothing the life path of her human companions. This message she herself titled "TONI TALKS."

TONI TALKS

"Today we will focus on breathing. It's an important lesson that is one to be revisited as often as you can. You see, awareness same as breath, is what keeps you closest to the truth—the way through and to any dream, desire, or fulfillment. The breath is yours. See it calm you. Feel it ground you. You are one with the universe, in the All, when you are aware of your breath.

Today, as you move about the planet, think of your breath. Feel how differently you sense your motion and interactions. See with your 'soul eyes' and every question will have an answer and your way will be clearly depicted. It's about getting to calmness but more significantly it is about connecting to knowing. You will know what you seek when you are aware of your breath.

It is hoped you will practice your own 'being in the moment.'

Leave the trivia and angst just hovering over your shoulder and choose the white bright energy of joy and rightness. You have free will and each moment spent in fruitless railing against injustices or hurt take away from your life force, your opening into the quiet strength of the love of the All. Brush away the non-positive, send your healing energy out and ask for others to be protected and cared for. The animals are your guides in this. Watch them. Know their ability to help and forgive. They carry no anger day to day but live in the moment of godliness."

PHOEBE

Lastly a beautiful and serene female Elephant Ear Beta by the name of Phoebe brings more spiritual awareness of being in the moment and living a life chosen with intention and full of love. Her young mistress, Jennifer, loves her dearly and is becoming an accomplished psychic reader herself.

Communication scribed by Tina Marie Gancarz

Phoebe's Message
January 22, 2022

"I am a fully aware being. I have chosen this seemingly short 'lifetime' but it presents such richness. I have been spending at least 10 lifetimes in a row as a domestic fish. Once a crab, that felt so odd, and boring after a bit. I missed the graceful float. I do so appreciate a fully aware human in the household. So liberating to have another KNOW that this is a continuum. The in and out and option for diversity in the return. Truly splendid as a fish.

Funny. You would think it dull and minimal or sad from a human viewpoint. But I would encourage you to try a turn as a fish sometime, or get into meditation with one of us knowings. We really have a deep connection to spirit. Peace in the minimalist life. Think of the humans that get close to achieving this Zen state. And then know it can not compare or come close to what we experience all day every day.

I may seem relatively young to you but I am in my prime. Life moves swiftly for us. In and out, back and gone here and there. Swiftly. Yes. And that is part of the joy of it for us. Doesn't get too messy. Easy outs. And maybe sometime in spirit but mostly we just jump right back in and enjoy the ride again.

It's a ride. A grand grandiose safe peaceful ride. Might seem dull from there but trust me that it is exactly perfect for our kind. We are the 'jumpers.' Spirit aware. Short life beings. In and out. Suits us.

There is no sadness about our alleged passing as we are back in the living sometimes before you notice we are gone. Waste not the sadness for the escape, the exit. It's in perfect timing always. It's always exactly as we direct.

I will remain for a duration longer. I am not one fin out the door. I look forward to connecting directly. Showing you more about this and the universe. I have full connection and can be a source of great knowledge in your questing.

I am content to just be. Or to be a source. I am here in layers. As a companion for you foremost. I take great pride in this. But I have the capacity to be as much and more as you like.

I share my peace filled energy with you now. (pause). It carries the essence of purple. Yes. You felt that. It is rich, calming, sufficient. I am offering this at any time that you wish. I have a stream endlessly of this energy and honored to share. I am content.

That is my message for Spirit Being Jennifer."

CHAPTER 4

Sacred Soul Contracts— The Divine Purposes Of Animals

Each human creates their own Sacred Soul Contract or "blueprint" before they return to the physical plane from the spiritual plane. This blueprint can be described as a Divine Plan for the unfolding of life experiences of the highest potential for that spirit. It directs us to a perfect state of consciousness and can enable the awareness of our own "old memories" that lie deep within each of us as we traverse the present life. The blueprint is a part of the Akashic Records of the past, present, and future of all things in all dimensions, known and unknown. More information is available in many books and articles.

    Although many humans recognize their animal companions on the physical plane as only pets or working or show animals, these creatures are much, much more and have their own unique blueprints for this lifetime. They exist at all times in the spiritual plane, both while alive and after death. The horsemen of the Lakota Native American peoples acknowledge the eternal existence their horses; the horse represents the spiritual realm. A horse is painted with symbols, reminders of this to their guardians. A circle is painted around the eye because he is the bridge between the physical and the spiritual realm. Man cannot see the spiritual realm but the horse's eye can and through him, man understands and sees. Likewise three horizontal parallel coup marks are drawn on the face, rump, and legs representing from bottom to top— the spirit, the physical being, and Creator of all creation—all together in one, just as is the horse.

All animals vibrate energetically in their spiritual beings on a very high angelic level and as such they can act as the bearers of profound spiritual messages for humans. They are prompters of insightful soul growth using their gentle nudging because they act as guardians and protectors of a human's divine blueprints. Being guardians of our soul blueprints is a role of great importance and sacrifice for our animal companions and one that is not taken lightly. They see us as their life's intention, one of teaching and of total devotion. A companion animal is most happy and satisfied when they have helped us "go within," to be relaxed in higher awareness, and show progress along our own individual paths.

Certainly pets (and all living creatures) have their own life contracts to develop and realize, but their close ties to the spiritual level allows them to help us while continuing their own development. The animals are masters at their role and are divinely creative in their work.

The most astounding and beloved aspect here is that each human and animal chose to draw up a mutual Divine Contract while still in the spiritual realm before arriving back to this earthly existence. In fact, many animals and humans have been together through past lifetimes, always by their own agreement. It is an expression of divine universal love and acceptance by the animal that allows both human and animal to share in that love and to grow each in their own path.

Guardians often ask how many past lifetimes they have shared with their pet of today. The explanation is a bit shadowy, almost a mist, that is a complicated interweaving of spirits. As a lovely tabby cat once described to me:

KITANA (See more of her messages in Chapter 5)
August 29, 2019

"It is more a conglomerate, a gathering of energies, separate at times, joined at others. Our entwined 'souls' are more intricate than a 'past shared lifetime.' Rather, there is a higher level than just the 'physical' when sharing, mixing, separating and swirling back together and it is an ongoing, extremely ancient working that has occurred in spiritual before we choose to return to the physical for the time to do the experiencing and sharing as planned. All is as it should be."

Know too that our companion animals now crossed over continue their work with us, never leaving us, always around us. I once was a presenter at a psychic fair when an attendee who had never met me walked over and said, "Do you know you have a whole roomful of animals behind you?" Yes, I did, because just so, I am always protected and guided by these spirits.

Animals fully understand their purpose and stay continuously connected with the Universal All and with each other. A mother cat losing her kittens to adoption stays spiritually connected to each of those kittens, recognizing the life plan of each kitten and her own purpose, and the completion of the life cycle. They share unconditional love among themselves and understand each kitten is leaving to new homes for the start of another experience, another opportunity to teach and heal.

In my many psychic readings with animals, they will address their guardians' concerns and explain their health and behavior issues because they are truly also a cat or a dog or a horse or whichever form they have chosen to experience in this lifetime. Additionally, companion animals can describe past lives shared with their human family. Most profoundly, an animal companion often will move to loving spiritual messages for their human companions, urging them perhaps to become more enlightened, to be creative, to meditate, or to live in the moment, for example. These lessons are of contemplation, of learning to grieve a loss while gaining the strength and wisdom for having had that loss, and of experiencing love of warmth and total non-judgmental acceptance of another being. And lastly, they are so very strong in sending vibrational energy to their guardians, allowing enlightenment that the Great Unknown is around and within each of us, down to the tiniest atom. Sharing this can prompt humankind to communicate better with the animal kingdom through the unspoken psychically intuitive language of "knowing."

So spend more time in meditation, slow down a little bit, and consciously choose to "smell the roses," be one with the sunsets and sunrises, be enchanted with all of life. Ask your pets why and how their behaviors are trying to teach you something. If you do not oblige, your pets will surely try even harder to awaken you to what is needed. There is nothing so stark as a pet jumping onto your chest at 2 AM!

TINKERBELLE

Tinkerbelle, a tiny female chihuahua who disappeared 4 yrs previously was still being grieved by her guardian, Kecia. Her reading with me exemplifies the compassion, healing, and spiritual messages for growth coming from the other side.

TINKERBELLE'S MESSAGE
SEPTEMBER 5, 2019

Tinkerbelle, may I do this session at this time with you, communicating at the highest level and good for all. (Asking permission honors the unique being of each spirit.)

TINKERBELLE. "Yes, Ma, of course." (All the animals call me Ma.)

She comes forward to me in a tunnel of white light and love, prancing, wiggling her hips as she walks, coming to sit in front of me.

Tinkerbelle, how are you doing just now?

TINKERBELLE. "Oh, Ma. So wonderfully spiritually fine. I live in a delirium of love, delightfully light and airy, no aches, no pains of old age for me. I float a few feet off the ground in front of my Mum. I zip up into the tops of trees to see the glory of all the things around my Mum. I rip and race, snort and bark just as I did in my physical body."

Your Mum is grieving for you still after 4 yrs of your disappearance. Can you tell me how I might help her with that sadness?

TINKERBELLE. "Of course, Ma. The problem here is that my dearest Mum doesn't know I am around her still—every waking and sleeping moment. My energy vibration is brought to her, hovering, surrounding, healing, taking away burdens that she does not need to carry anymore. Can you please tell my Mum I am with her, truly I am? She need only take a deep breath, relax, and ask me to make myself known to her. She will see sparkles of glitter in the air. She will hear my familiar bark.

All is well. Really it is. My Mum now needs to heed my message of healing—healing her heart and opening it to new beginnings, new chances, new progression, in her spiritual journey.

It is true we shared our pathways for 5 years. We planned that before we both returned to the physical from the spiritual. We mapped it out—the experiences we wanted to share so we could BOTH grown on our path. That is—joy, deep sorrow, encumbrances and revolt, repair and regeneration, love, tears, happiness, despair. We planned it all— for the greatest good was gained by our sharing of these intimacies, these secret and not-so-secret nestlings and hugs and sweet words of wisdom and adoration.

Please ask my Mum if this isn't true. Can she see the great leaps of faith and 'knowing' that we developed in 5 short years? Ask her to acknowledge this great spiritual growth. I am positively quivering, waiting for her to see and allow the light and energy of the All, the Universe, to bathe her, soothe her, prepare her for her next steps in this life. It was necessary that I leave as I did for all these reasons."

Tinkerbelle, can you tell me how it happened when you disappeared four years ago?

TINKERBELLE. "Yes, Ma. It was so quick, lightening fast. Here one second, gone the next. My Mum is not to cry over my crossing. It is as I planned it, what I wanted to experience. I saw a dark cloud just over me before it happened—a snatching, so to speak. I did not see the animal to describe it to you. But it was as it should have been.

Now, can we progress onto something more special, more endearing, more entrancing, more lovely? I am readying myself to return to the physical in a little while. (I was shown Christmas lights against a dark sky.). I am choosing to return as a small dog again. Considered a cat but wanted to be a dog in my Mum's life again. Tell her I will be a small black ball of fur—and she will fall in love with me instantly. Valentine's Day of Love will be around the time she finds me, I find her. It will be in the most unexpected place. She will be 'gobsmacked,' totally surprised and delighted.

As she grows, she will see some of my 'Tinkerbelle' mannerisms which I choose to keep with me in this life time—-happy attitude, totally trusting of my Mum, and loving to play (I was shown tug-of-war with a toy.). I will sit by her side and be absolutely enthralled by the TV as it plays, watching the action back and forth across the screen.

I will bring my Mum so much freshness and happiness. But I ask in return that she fulfills her end of the bargain—to lay aside all grieving for me this fall when the leaves change, to open herself to the splendid joy and excitement of life, the sacred air and sacred water and sacred earth and sacred fire, to relish the beauty of the rising sun and rustling of the leaves in the trees, to relish the sparkly glint in a dewdrop, to smell the morning fog. In short, to 'live' and be grateful for all that sustains her, surrounds her, gives her beauty.

In that way, my Mum will prepare herself for me to return. This is how it must be for us to mesh, share, grow and live in this new pathway of shared love. Can you tell her these things, Ma?"

Yes, Tinkerbelle, I will tell her all you have said.

TINKERBELLE. "I am so grateful to you, Ma, for this chance to reach my Mum, to talk to her, to explain things, to help her heal from her grief of my unexpected disappearance. Please tell her I am so very excited for our reunion. The Universe is preparing for this to happen in all love and light. I have asked Archangel Michael to come to my Mum at this time as he is the 'Protector of Joy' and will surround her with his perfect vibration as he watches over her.

Thank you, Ma. That is all. Go in Peace."

There is yet another amazing connection through our soul contracts with animals. Animals find their guardians and new homes and not the other way around, though some people might believe otherwise. An animal will make a great effort to be with its family-to-be. How often does the stray kitten or dog arrive on the back step only to adopted into its forever home. How does the spark of an animal at a rescue cause the human to instantly be attracted to them, to know them even when the adopter had a very different envisioning?

These are not chance encounters. Synchronicity of the Divine Spirit was planned long before these two physical manifestations, human and animal, met and bonded. The blueprint was created between the two spirits describing how they would help one another, what lessons and elevations of loving energy would be achieved, and how long they needed to share their lives. These plans, these angelic projections, these needed growing of experiences and higher vibrations are the bases of the family formed by people and animals.

Do not doubt these intentions were completed, though in future moments there may be sadness, guilt, or feelings of unfulfilled sharing due to separation. Trust always in these sacred unfolding connections that are for the highest good for all.

HARLEY

Here is a lovely example of a session I had with Harley, a four-year old German Pointer female dog, who was adopted from a shelter after her previous owner died. Her earliest life was unknown. Her present guardian, Nancy, had concerns that she was somewhat grouchy to a sister dog in the home, she becomes agitated when a shovel was brought out to pick up poop, jumping and barking and going crazy, and she had issues with shadows when the sun was setting, always looking for the shadows to chase and bark at. The family had much love for her and wanted to understand her and what she had gone through in the past so that they could work with her to make her life with them as happy as possible.

HARLEY'S MESSAGE
January 2, 2020

Harley, may I speak with you at this time?

HARLEY. "Sure, Ma. What's the topic of conversation?"

Well, Harley, we might start by my asking how you are doing just now.

HARLEY. "Fine, Ma. Really feeling fine, fit-as-a-fiddle, mellow, happiness seeping into all parts of my body. Kinda like what you might call meditation but light, lovely, bubbly, wondrous. Do you know what I mean?"

I do know. It is that joyous being—not dwelling on the ponderous whys of life. Am I sensing you correctly, Harley?

HARLEY. "Spot on, Ma. It is just such a great, joyous time to be alive—bam, bang, hippity-hop energy. I am so happy, so so happy."

Your Mum has some things she is wanting to ask you about. First of all, how was your life before you came to your Mum?

HARLEY. "Well, at first I was frightened when I was alone as a little puppy. I was alone in a pen and I cried and barked but there was really no one to help me. I got more scared when it got dark and I could hear all the others dogs barking.

They were lonely too. Then a man came to take me to a new place. It was OK in that I was warm and fed and petted but something was missing—kind of like an emptiness in that man. I comforted him at times but it was soon time for him to return to the spiritual. Pretty soon I was in another cage and feeling alone again."

Can you tell me why you get agitated and bark and jump when your family gets out the shovel to scoop up poop in the yard?

HARLEY. "Oh, that was my play time, my connect-with-human time, when my pen was cleaned. The shovel meant a sort-of play time. Sometimes it was a game to move away and toward the shovel, sometimes the person got upset. I was just so happy to see someone and it didn't matter if they disapproved of my jumping and barking. You know I am a very people-person dog. I came in this life to BE with my human family, to bond, to share love, to play and sleep, to rock-and-roll in exuberance sometimes."

Harley, do you think you still need to regard a shovel as play-time with jumping and barking? Do you think that maybe when the shovel is brought out you might like to play by chasing a ball while the shovel is being used?

HARLEY. "Well, no one has ever played with me at that time. I just made up my own play time. But chasing a ball or running in play with a person might be really fun. Could you tell my Mum?"

Harley, I will tell her. Do you think you can temper and quiet your reaction to the shovel in this way?

HARLEY. "I will try really hard, Ma. I didn't know it was upsetting my family."

Your family only wants you to be happy and feel loved and contented, dear one. Your Mum would like to know why you chase shadows, particularly at sunset, Harley.

HARLEY. "Well, Ma, being caged all the time when I was young and alone, I made up my own games. And when I saw my shadow moving, it was like a rabbit chase game. It kept me going and helped work off my energy. Does my family want me to quit that too?"

Harley, I don't think they want you to quit with your game. They were just so very concerned that you were behaving in an odd way. Would you like your family to join in with you, make shadows with their bodies that you could chase all around.

HARLEY. "Well, wouldn't that be fun? We would all be laughing and giggling while we do it. The earth needs so much fun and laughter just now, don't you think?"

Yes, Harley, that is a lovely, happy thought. Your Mum would also like to understand why you are aggressive with Riley (sister dog) at times? Do you know why you do that?

HARLEY. "I don't want to have to share with her all the time. My toys, my pets-on-the-head, my food—these are mine to keep and protect."

Harley, this makes your Mum feel very uneasy and sad. She would really like you to be kind and caring to your sister, Riley. Yes, you have your toys and food and attention from humans. But do you not think there is enough to go around, to share, to wait your turn at times. Being kind to Riley is a compromise of sorts so that you can live in a warm, loving, happy home that takes everyone into the light of acceptance.

HARLEY. "Well, I never thought about that. You know I have not had toys or food or pets at times in my life before and I feel I need to protect those when I get them. Riley is such a silly girl, so quiet and loving. She means me no harm. I know that. Now I must try really hard to harness my 'doggie pack' behavior. I can see that I can let go of that—right?"

Harley, it is your behavior that upsets your Mum so your behavior must be toned down to be sure she is content and happy. I think you do want that for your Mum and the rest of the family.

HARLEY. "I will try really hard, Ma. Guess you might call that mellowing out. I see that it will be much nicer for Riley and for me if I keep my 'feathers unfluffed.' "

Thank you for that, Harley. Your working on positive behavior will be nice for everyone. Harley, do you have anything else you would like to tell your Mum?

HARLEY. "Oh sure. Dear Mum—thank you for bringing me into this forever home. I am getting the gist of what it is like to be in a steady, calm, loving, routine-like life. It steadies me and brings me into my highest self. But know that in addition to my happy bouncy self which brings her smiles, and my loving warmth which makes her happy, I also bring energy for her from the higher beings, the spirituals, you might say. I am helping her come into that consciousness of being each and every day. Perhaps she is noticing these little changes in herself, a deepening of love, an elevation of joy, a feeling of growing into her path. Please tell her that she can 'talk' to me about that anytime. I know and understand much more than she realizes. We share many lovely moments of this elevating energy of spirit. This will be become much more evident as we two trod along together. Ah, love is in the air, so to speak. All is as it should be."

Anything else, Harley?

HARLEY. "No, Ma. Go in peace."

And you also Harley.

GUS

And finally here is a brilliant love story from a reading with Gus, a six year old male Shitzu/terrier. His Mum, Lori, had concern both for his anxiety and not wanting to be left alone and for his nipping at men. Reading his words, please be aware of our conversation as it shifts from the physical being of Gus and his "doggie" struggles to the spirit being of Gus as he discusses divine sacred contracts so important to his shared life with his Mum at this time.

GUS'S MESSAGE
April 5, 2019

Gus, may I speak with you at this time?

GUS. "Yes, Ma."

He approached me through the tunnel of light and love between our two hearts, slowly with head down, then sat in front of me and started to crawl on his belly. I asked him to sit and be brave.

Earlier during his session as Gus was sent healing energy vibrations to assist him in adapting to change and releasing his emotion of anxiety, he showed himself standing facing toward and accepting this incoming energy. He then showed me his spirit bouncing up a little at a time on a trampoline, just above his body, as he practiced this new feeling.

Lastly I was shown that Gus's uncle (in spirit) on his father's side is with him at all times to offer his shoulder for support and to reduce Gus's timidity, shuddering, and fear. He is there to reinforce Gus's strength to go forward, completing some steps on his divine pathway. Uncle offers protection and a "place" for Gus to relax and regroup when he is upset and frightened.

How are you doing this evening, Gus?
GUS. "Oh, pretty good, Ma. And yourself?"

I am fine, Gus, and happy to be talking with you. Your Mum is quite worried about you and asked me to check in with you.

GUS. "Sure, Ma. I know already—don't bite the old men."
Could you tell me about that, Gus?

GUS. "These men are shadowy, angry. I am unable to know what is coming next. I am in a high state of alert, protecting my Mum."

How might we help you feel more calm about men coming near you?

GUS. "Well, could you ask my Mum to step out in front of me to show that man that she is the boss. Keep me behind her. She needs to be the "wolf pack leader" and then I can relax. She is in charge and I don't have to protect her or her territory. Can you ask my Mum to do that. We will need to P-R-A-C-T-I-C-E to retire the old 'native dog; neural pathways, so to speak. Can she do that, Ma?| Tell her to explain to me face-to-face? I need to hear it from her."

I will ask her, Gus, and I am sure she will work with you so you can be happy and calm again. Gus, do you think you are able to be left alone without your Mum?

GUS. "Well, it is very scary. Black box, all alone. What is happening to me. Where is she. Why doesn't she see my terror?"
Gus, would you be able to be left if you were in a big kennel, all open,

so you could see out?

GUS. "I dunno. For how long? Days, nights—all alone. Help. Where is everybody?"

Gus, would it help if your Mum explained why you have to be kenneled, where she is going, and how soon she will be back

GUS. "I dunno. Could we practice that a little? Can she talk to me, ask me to try it just for a little bit. I am mostly scared to be left because she won't come back ever. I think I can do this for her, but only little by little. I just want protection and her love at this time. As I heal, I will be able to love and protect her too, give her space, teach her how to laugh with me again. She is a lovely woman, you know. So full of giving.

My divine purpose in coming to her was to help her express her true self, to remember the depth of her spirituality as she helps so many others. Our pathways are not parallel but one path we share. The moon and stars light our way and the ancestors watch over us both. Tell my loving Mum not to despair. All is moving forward from the great lessons we have just learned. These were needed so that we could both express the love of Creator more fully, more joyfully, and with more awareness. I am here for her and she for me, love eternal.

That is all for now, Ma. Go in peace."

And you also, Gus.

Gus's Reading
November 21, 2019

This reading with Gus was quite unique in that he requested another reading with me some 8 months later by coming into a dream with his Mum where he was laying on her chest and he asked to have "that lady" talk to him again (which she immediately knew was me). This beautiful spirit-angel of mysticism needed to help his Mum in a very direct and immediate way by communicating to her through me. Here is what Gus had to say.

Gus, I am here to talk with you now. Can you tell me about your messages and feelings. Your Mum is anxious about her dream of you laying on her chest when you told her that you wanted to talk with "that lady" again. Your messages will put her heart to rest.

Gus. "Well, Ma. It's like this. I know you can tell my Mum what she needs to know. You will be my conduit—Okay?"

Sure, Gus.

Gus. "My Mum is my beloved and most trusted soul, the one I came to be with, to guide, to protect, to support. She is nearing a change in her life for which she must be prepared. She will do very well with this change and it has to do with the heart energies. But she must look ahead, know exactly what is waiting there, be prepared for a different path than what she might now be considering.

I am here to warn her of the many vagaries, the skullduggery, the dangers in which she may find herself. She needs to surround herself with her most trusted and loving friends and family. Do not take her eyes off them for a second, stay close to them, hold hands and hearts. Be prepared. Together is strength. Never be alone. Keep trusted ones close by.

I do not send this message for Mum to frighten her but to 'gird her loins' for the changes that are coming. In that way, I smooth the path for her, light the path on all sides with brilliant illumination, so the way is clear and lucid and all is as it should be.

She needs to know and remember that I am by her side at every moment. I am not just her 'pet' but I am her strong guardian angel. I came to protect her and protect her I will. Please ask my Mum to become cognizant of the meditations she now needs to begin. It is time to move into that higher level of 'knowing.' She begins that path by meditating, seeing the overall wholeness of everything that is. In that way, she begins to enlarge heart and soul into becoming one with all that is.

I cannot stress enough that she needs to begin these new lessons now. There are meditations to listen to on the internet, white candles to burn, quiet, quiet music to bring in the proper energies. She must learn the cleansing quality of smudging with sage smoke, learning to ground herself and asking spiritual to take all non-positive energies from her to the center of the earth to be transmuted into love.

Thus it is that it is time for my Mum to move into the circles of like-minded spiritual light workers who bring the healing energies to all levels of being, in all times, in all spaces. My Mum has known this intuitively all her life but has had lessons to experience before beginning this new journey. Again, please assure her that all her loving thoughts and energies are known, her guardians and angels and higher beings surround her and enclose her in their loving arms. She is stirred and swirled and given the laughter and joy and high-spirited dancing of the souls—and I am right there with her.

As she meditates, I will be bringing new and beautiful messages to her. I come as her friend, her mentor, her beloved of times past, present, and future. She need only call me in and we are instantly of one energy, one beautiful beam of light, one 'heavenly' love. As I said and I will repeat, my Mum has known this all her life and now it is time to allow doors to open, windows to illuminate, hearts to sing."

Anything else, Gus?

Gus. "No, Ma. Thank you for helping me bring these messages to my Mum. I am every grateful. Go in peace."

And I am likewise honored to have been of help, Gus. Go in peace also.

Understanding and wanting to experience greatest possibilities of sharing your life with an animal is the most loving of intentions. It leads to connection to the Great Unknown, the One Source, Creator, wherein one may be shown a bright and clear picture, a pathway, a message of mysticism. But that image, that knowing, does not imply manifestation is imminent without trust for the unspreading of that image in the time and space for your highest good and wellbeing.

Animals through their Divine Contract choices may be with you for 20 years or a day or just a fleeting moment but the encounter is to help teach and illuminate and expand the blossoming of soul awareness. If you live in the moment, become aware, pay attention to these loving animal-sharing happenings, the fullness of your soul will burst with the new knowledge, the expressivity of creation, the utter acceptance of the grace of the Universal Source.

CHAPTER 5

Animals As Protectors, Healers, Sources of Laughter and Bliss

THE SENTRY

The sentry prowls the polished halls
While the temple settled and slept.
Shadows slither along its walls
And outside the darkness wept.

His blue eyes probe the darkness deep,
His cat paws whisper only.
Candles glow in the idols' keep.
But the sentry is not lonely.

Shadow people from hidden worlds
Stroke the sentry's whiskers long.
He smiles and purrs as incense curls,
He murmurs soft their song.

None enter here, this hallowed hall.
Few know its secret buried past.
But the sentry knows its silent call,
His task lies here, his lot is cast.

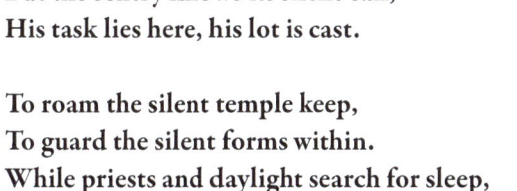

To roam the silent temple keep,
To guard the silent forms within.
While priests and daylight search for sleep,
The sentry's ageless task begins.

   –LINDA BELLES

Part 1

Our ageless sentries, the animals spirits from the angelic realm, watch over us all, in tasks small and large. Their protection seamless and love unbroken, they faithfully guide and teach and heal us in this physical world full of vagaries and obstacles and illnesses. Though we each chose such experiences for a lifetime of soul growth, it is through our pets, those guardian angels, that we navigate our lives more calmly, more warmly, more strongly, for the tasks ahead.

The energy healing and protection by our animals occurs in two ways which are actually intertwined as one. The first is their loving effects on the physical body, emotions, and diseases of humans and other animals. They do these with tail wags, meows, neighs, barking at danger, happy playfulness, cuddling and loving kisses. An older brother cat may constantly groom and sleep with a genetically impaired cat lacking mental acuity, vision and gait and unable to groom and keep its fur clean. Ukrainian soldiers adopting abandoned dogs in war zones are repaid by the dogs growling when strangers approach or even a few minutes before bombs come raining down on the troops. A dog may drop a pine cone at the feet of a guardian feeling sad. A cat purring in your lap is so comforting because the feelings are of pure love and contentment.

The second is the equally strong process of animals healing others—their guardians, other humans, other animals. They use their psychic connection to the One Source to act as a conduit bringing healing vibrational energies to the recipient's body. They can do this telepathically close up or at a distance. We are all one. The sender is always connected to the being receiving the help. All of this is happening outside of time which is not fixed or linear and there is no separation. Obviously all humans are capable of doing the same because the God Force is within all—every being, every cell, every molecule, even those who have crossed over.

Sometimes animals are so intent on healing their humans, they will take on the disease themselves. It is common for pets develop the same disease as their guardians, from diabetes to rare heart tumors, to itchy paws in response to neuropathy of feet, and more.

Animal energy human workers are always aware of the power of the work being done and never underestimate what can be accomplished. We never forget we are working in flowing dimensions, universes, of time. We can easily go back and forward as we work in the present. A healing team of guides and angels and archangels, both of the animal healer and of the animal itself, go ahead and pave the way and begin the healing before a session even begins. They monitor to keep the healing effects at the best level—not too much and not too little. Thus we are partnering with the divine, opening and allowing the amazing sacred energy, to flow through us as conduits, allowing that transfer of healing energy through us.

Guardians and animal communicators alike can be opened up to the spiritual nature of their animals that is bound to their own spiritual growth. Recognizing your own spiritual being and the spiritual beings of animals brings you to a child-like space of open heart and open mind where you can be at your highest frequency of vibrational energy. Learn from the animals to laugh and be playful. The old souls of animals are playful and recognize that wonderful energy vibration. We are all pure spirits but animals always and easily say, "I am here. I am full of love." Everything is fine as they live in happiness and carry on, adapting easily as they so ably release the past. They truly are of the angelic realm.

No one spirit or soul is higher or lower in any aspect—beauty, acuity, devotion, creativity, giving of self. Each is an extraordinary being, an individual so unique it will never exist in this same physical form again. An ant is as beautiful as a newborn human baby, as needed on the earth and in the universe as any archangel. Be humble regarding your own place with the All. Do not doubt for a moment that animals or even trees are lower forms of beings, dumb animals, unknowing plants. This attitude only diminishes your own energy and the closed mind hinders your own uprising of being in the light. To understand, absorb, and relish stories of animal communications and healings—that is, animal mysticism— requires your commitment to a profound belief that we are as one, "all my relatives."

Create yourself for every living being the acts of kindness that can grow into the universal love and bring your being into vibrational synchrony with the highest love. For, after all, this is what animals do with and for us. They create and intend their healing energy be brought in shimmering trails of mysticism to be understood as the beautiful power of unconditional acceptance, unlimited love, and energy healing. They infuse these into each and every person they encounter. Know too that this caring and showing of love and protection exists after an animal crosses over.

Therefore, animals like people exist at two levels, one of which is the doggie or kitty self who comes to experience life as a dog or cat. They have emotions of joy, sadness, grief at loss of a companion, pain, fear, love, and caring. They are, however, masters of living in the now. At a second level, the animals act at a much higher energy vibration. They have a soul, a spiritual self. They are spirits who choose to descend to earth to both experience life in the physical body and to lovingly help others. They come to be helpers, healers, guides, and lovers of all things pure and good to allow humans to experience nonjudgmental acceptance and true brilliant love from another sentient being. They give a human soul those unfolding and soarings of spirit needed. Life in the physical is only a playground, a library, a swift water raft ride, a nursing of an aging parent—a continuum of being—which offers ways to share, be present, give love. For all that matters is the loving act, however small, which never leaves, never is forgotten, is always part of the whole which is the All, the Great Unknown. So too in these two levels of animal and human existence is the essence of communicating with animals at both levels simultaneously.

PART 2

As a teacher, inventor, leader, healer, explorer, pathfinder, and creative spirit, you are given by the animals that protective energy and smoothing warmth you need to develop physically, emotionally, and spiritually. When you seek to be more aware of the way you live and deliberately follow pure living in the path of higher consciousness, you will develop your life purposes which you, all along, have intended.

Think of the many examples where animals bring you to that higher energy. They bring stress reduction by their humorous playfulness and examples of total relaxation. They show alternatives to anger and non-positive energies of emotion. They bring energy healing in sickness. They show altruism by sharing and being protective of others. They bring messages of compassion if you are willing to listen. You are being offered lessons in kindness, acceptance, forgiveness and caring. These are all acts of pure love from the animals. In return, give them love and abundant gratefulness and hugs, lots and lots of hugs.

Here are three such instructive messages to guardians. Again please note the the animals call me "Ma" and they call their guardians "Mum."

TONI JO'S MESSAGE (SEE TONI JO, CHAPTER 3)
JUNE 12, 2018

"Sometimes you run for your loved ones. This is not a lifetime of conveniences. It is a celebration of energy. It's a time when we do for one another simply because we love them. It can cost us: other. Have each other's backs. Love drives it all. Love is the reason we do. It's love."

KITANA

Kitana is a tabby female cat, an adopted rescue, of about 7 years old, living with her beloved guardian, Laurie.

Animals As Protectors, Healers,
Sources of Laughter and Bliss

KITANA'S MESSAGES TO HER GUARDIAN, LAURIE, ON THEIR SHARED LIVES
SEPTEMBER 24, 2019

Kitana, will you please come forward?

Kitana. "Sure, Ma." (She comes gracefully, tail held high.)

May I speak with you at this time?

Kitana. "I am here for you, Ma. What's up?"

Your Mum wanted me to check back in with you. Is that OK with you, Kitana?

Kitana. "Sure, Ma. Let's try to go a few steps further on in our relationship. First of all, I am not going to "get lost." This is my forever beautiful home and I choose to stay right where I am. I'd much rather have a tree house to hang out in—up high so I can look out. Maybe a few fake leaves to pretend I am the great cat hunter watching for prey from my hidey-hole. So much fun to curl up high and above. Even better in front of a window to watch the world go by—maybe even a few chirpies (she shows me small birds) to keep me entertained"

(She is now showing me a CD player —and I am getting the words "meditation music"). Is this something, Kitana, you would like your Mum to use, to get used to, familiar with, as she frees her abilities in communicating with you?

Kitana. "Yes, Ma. She needs to get her energy aligned, smooth, quiet. In that way, she can ask me a question and I can send her an answer. Her intention is so important. If this is what she wants between us, then she must fervently wish, no—intention with her mind. It must come from her heart. That is where she will feel the opening of the fire, the light, the love between us as it begins to flow in telepathy.

Please tell my my Mum to not stop trying —all is there for her to dip into as she begins this path of higher knowing. I am with her every moment as are all of her own guides and angels. They all wish her to succeed as do I."

Anything else, Kitana?

Kitana. "No, Ma. Go in peace."

And you also, Kitana.

KITANA'S SECOND MESSAGE
NOVEMBER 16, 2021

May I speak with you at this time, Kitana?

Kitana. "Certainly, Ma."

Your Mum would like me to check in with you to see how you are doing and if you have any messages for her.

Kitana. "Well, here goes, Ma. Please tell my Mum all is good on my end of things here at our home. It is an eclectic kind of life here and never a dull moment. I like the energy and healing and happy times though there may be interludes of sadness and down energy. That is perfectly OK in my perspective. Each day is a step up—never down. Some steps steeper than others. Some steps just an easy glide over the door-sill.

So I don't get upset when the long view is ahead of me at all times. I set my own life path and my Mum and Zeus (her brother cat) and I decided while still in the spiritual together how we would share and what we would learn as we came together as a 'group' family in the physical. All is as it should be, moving apace in time—sometimes giant leaps, sometimes baby steps, sometimes just stepping cadence in time without a forward movement. Each effort and work, of course, is a creation, a mirror of love, a knowing of tolerance and absolute love and acceptance without reservation.

Sometimes the human spirit forgets these spiritual contracts, these plans made in spirit before coming back into the physical bodies of this lifetime. But we animals, coming from a higher angelic vibration, never forget, never lose track of the goals and aims set so long ago. We bring the steadiness, the absolute forgiveness, the brightness and love of the spirit that becomes known to humans totally after crossing the rainbow bridge. We animals carry it with us at all time. We are the healers and teachers of the humans. Our love is deep and everlasting and without boundaries.

This is the message I bring forth for my Mum. So, dear Mum, all is well, all is content, all is lovely. Don't you agree?"

Anything else, Kitana?

Kitana. "No, Ma. Go in peace and I am grateful to you for speaking with me. It is a lovely sharing we have had. Go in peace."

Thank you Kitana. I am grateful. Go in peace also.

SPARKY

Sparky is a 9 year old female golden retriever who was a guide dog from Guide Dogs for the Blind for his guardian Mum who has some balance problems as does Sparky himself. He is now retired and living with her.

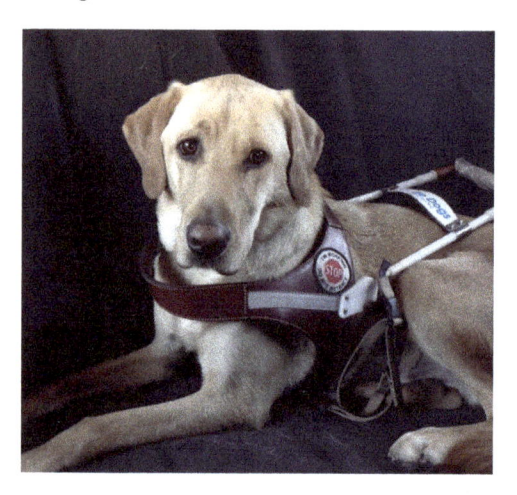

SPARKY'S MESSAGES
SEPTEMBER 7, 2019

Sparky, may I speak with you at this time?

SPARKY. "Yes, Ma. Glad you are here. I want to speak to you."

I am here, dear one. How are you doing today?

SPARKY. "Well, so-so. Feeling a bit better. Life is something, isn't it? One thing, then another, but beautifully moving forward to the loving end where all is congealed, spread, bumped, bounced, scattered out and in, always moving with the energy and love of the All. You do know that, Ma. Can you tell my Mum? She really does know too, but forgets sometimes in all the busy bustling of her life."

Can you tell me about your achiness and slow movement, Sparky?

SPARKY. "It is like a foggy space, Ma. Comes and goes. I don't know why but try my best to continue on as spiritedly as I can."

Can you tell me, from your higher self, if there is anything your Mum can to to help you with this?

SPARKY. "No, Ma. It is a necessary affliction of sorts as I absorb some of her dizziness and imbalance. She is much better, safer, with me near her. This is what I chose, to be with her, soothe her, protect her. She has done so very much to try to help my physical ailments and I am so grateful for her love and caring. But please tell her that our shared afflictions of balance and achiness at times are just that—SHARED. Our spirits know what it is to experience these things and because we SHARE, we also SOAR. The depth and height of our affection and love allows both of us to reach those beautiful goals we chose before returning to this lifetime. Hey girl, we chose 'good,' didn't we? I am so happy and peaceful as the days move on. My Mum is too. All is as it should be.

Ask my Mum to check my eyes—stare and stare again. She will see the spark of life, of love, of puppydom, of working dog, of old age and transformation. Each is in me and all is me. She will grow in wisdom, knowing, accepting, and embracing this knowing."

Anything else, Sparky?

SPARKY. "No, Ma. Go in peace."

And you also, Sparky.

SPARKY'S SECOND MESSAGE
APRIL 7, 2020

Sparky, I am grateful to help you with the energy and love of the All that comes through me to you. (I am shown a semicircle of yellow labs, all with guide dog harnesses, sitting around Sparky at this time. They are telling him it is OK to be tired and to relinquish his work obligations and responsibilities which he chose to take on in this life time. They tell him he has been a "good lad" who has gone the extra mile in trying to help the humans in his life. It is OK for him to step into the next phase of his life as he has now different lessons to share with the humans in his life. Their love and devotion and honoring of Sparky brings tears to me as I am being shown what a lovely soul he is—steady, good, uncomplaining, loving, and devoted to his work.)

Animals As Protectors, Healers, Sources of Laughter and Bliss

How are you feeling today, Sparky?

SPARKY. "A bit tired, Ma. I know my Mum is worried about this. I do not see that there is anything to be done at this time. Tell her, please, I am in no great pain. Just tired and 'elderly feeling.' I certainly am not feeling the zest of a young dog. It is more like it is time for me to relax in the sun and watch the world go by. It is comforting for me to have my Mum so near to me. Please tell her not to worry—all will be fine, just as fore-planned. My love for her shines through these eyes and I feel the extreme healing of her energies of love and concern. Please tell my Mum to just relax and enjoy the sun with me. Let's sit outside and soak in the sun, she with her tea and me with my blankie. Isn't that just a scene you can picture, Ma? Right out of a Normal Rockwell painting, I think. So much calm and inwardness, that is, living in the moment. That is what I think the two of us need at this time. My Mum is well aware of this and now she knows I am aware of it too. Our needs as we age are simpatico. No fuss—just slowing down and feeling our spirit energies soaring into those higher vibrations of grace and love."

Anything else, Sparky.

SPARKY. "No, Ma. Go in peace."

And you also, Sparky.

SPARKY'S THIRD MESSAGE
SEPTEMBER 4, 2021

May I speak with you at this time, Sparky?

SPARKY. Sure, Ma.

How are you doing just now?

SPARKY. "Just fine. I do enjoy these cool sunny days and listening to the birds overhead. They have so much, and I do mean much, to say. Without my harness and concentration of work and responsibility, I have much time to absorb all these conversations. Of course, I put in my two-cents worth too. The birds are deep into spiritual healing at this time—the earth, the well-being of the living and non-living components. They speak and coordinate and plan and are confident in this beautiful time of healing to come. Ma, they want you to listen too. Your feathers you find at your feet are plentiful now—many messages of spirit coming to you, many pleas for your loving energy to be sent in this healing. Listen to the songs and chirps and honks —even the "talk" of your little Chickie girl (my black hen). Absorb, codify, be strong in intent for this beautiful world to clean and clear and brighten and heal. Your intentions are most needed at this very time."

Thank you, Sparky. Yes, of course, I will be active in this light work. Sparky, your Mum would like to know how you are feeling without having to do harness guide dog work now.

Animals As Protectors, Healers, Sources of Laughter and Bliss

SPARKY. "Oh, please do tell my Mum that all is good. The bonds of responsibility built into my life's work have been released and I am satisfied to be by her side—physically, emotionally, and spiritually. The two of us have learned many lessons, have we not? Just as we planned for this lifetime. We have been there for each other —and we will continue this devotion. I am happy and light and I send thanks to my Mum for honoring my service dog work with her celebration of my retirement. It was much fun.

And now that all the festivities (of his retirement party) are over, let us relax and smile and be so very grateful for each other—as ever we were. Life is good, dear Mum."

Anything else, Sparky?

SPARKY. "No, Ma. Go in peace."

And you also, Sparky.

And so these examples show us the protection, healing, and encouragement of animals for their guardians in a wide array of ways. Love comes in many forms but none more devoted, compassionate, and unconditional than from our very own pets.

CHAPTER 6

Spiritual Guidance Through the Teachings of the Animals

The sepharic spirit or higher self of an animal comes as a gift to the earth and to humans, acting always in unconditional love as a teacher and as a healer. Animals bring the Universal Consciousness of the All.

Having psychic mediumship ability, they can understand our minds, read our thoughts, and know our heart's intents and spiritual energy. Directly tied to this is their ability to understand any spoken verbal language.

Some of the biggest lessons from our animal friends are forgiveness, non-judgmental love, and release. We can't love and aren't in love frequency, when we are blaming and judging. Comparing ourselves to others is always a thief of joy. We must learn to trust the Divine Source. The higher realm never misleads or mistreats.

Recognize that these loving creatures come to guide and heal our sad hearts, our feelings of isolation and lack of love, and even our poor health. Know that these animals are of high frequency energy from the angelic realm; they are universal spiritual guides who listen to our needs and give a helping hand to our internal soul and intuition. Love is always their message as they teach us how to trust the Source and know absolutely that Spirit never lies.

Some of the repeated teachings and messages in my psychic readings that have come from animals for both their guardians and for all of humanity include—

- non-judgmentally loving yourself and all beings
- being aware and living in the moment by becoming awed and inspired by each day
- learning to remain grounded and connected to the positiveness of the earth's energy
- trusting your intuition, your inner guidance
- meditating often to raise your positive vibrational energy and become receptive to the things being offered for your soul growth
- growing into yourself as a light being who has work to do of loving and healing others, in whatever form of bliss and creativity your heart offers up
- recognizing that all beings have intelligence and sentient wisdom, even to the tiniest of vibrational energies
- breathe in whole-heartedly to accept, and yearn to become, a part of the circle of life—life, death, and rebirth

Growing into these teachings is a way of bringing the energy of faithfulness, healing, and spiritual growth inwardly. Animals, particularly your very own pets, open your recognition and give reinforcement to your own innate abilities, those very things that bring you closer to the Divine Spirit. In other words, they help you develop trust in your abilities to expand your own spiritual and psychic path. You are given energy healing and spiritual growth both physically and emotionally. You are given the protection and warmth of the sacred light. By their companionship and example of unconditional acceptance and love of their human families, your companion animals help you be more aware of the way you act and think, deliberately choosing pure living in the path of higher consciousness. It is of the highest order for you to develop your life purposes for which you have chosen to experience and grow with in this lifetime.

You are being taught compassion, kindness, acceptance, forgiveness, and love in order to make that conscious evaluation of your intention before acting. These are all acts of pure love with which animals have chosen to help you. Give them the love and abundant gratefulness of your constant protection and hugs. Lots and lots of hugs.

And here are some of my own lessons scribed verbatim from my beloved animal relatives. As you read, you will see the variety of personalities and teachings each has brought to me. I am so very grateful for each and every one.

TONI JO (A BLACK LAB DOG)

JANUARY 13, 2018

"You have a message. You have work to do. Do not be discouraged at one aspect when so many are blooming right around your feet. Be joyful for the All's work sent to you. Every effort pushes you forward. Stern/ stiff back/ trust. Jingling of bells above you brings glittering light, a swelling of your heart's happiness. Crocodile welcomes you back to the ancient ones. We await you, but push you to swim through the sludge to the clear stream, the burbling brook, the sunlight dancing on the water. Many await your healing hands. Move forward and love, love, love."

HEINTZY (my adopted mix dog)—"Listen. Listen with your heart. Do you feel the incoming with your heart. Hold that feeling. Grow with it. I have come with things to teach you as I am also a healer filled with lessons of love."

KODA (my adopted collie mix dog)—"I come to protect you and I come to help you to know that everyday is a new day, fresh and one in which you and I need to look for fun."

JIGGS (a crossed-over dog)—"I am dog. I am man. I am one in all. You are here to help the animals but also to listen and know and become one with them all. They are yours; you are theirs.

Relax and believe in yourself. You are like an angel, white and with wings, floating and flying everywhere and nowhere at once. Remember you childhood gift of flying? You still fly and are free—to be and do all that you truly want. Time is of the essence for you to follow your path.

You are a caretaker and a nurturer. You help the four-leggeds in many ways but remember to listen to everything on your property, the trees and grass and wind, all the plants and winged ones, all the unseen little ones. Do not marvel but absorb and live and become one with each and all of them. Ask for your answers in your animal communication sessions and be sincere and loving in your search. Always know you are given the information you need to make decisions in your psychic light work. Look to the Star Nations and the ancestors for your guidance as they are with you always.

You have been told you are a child of the universe and so you are. Your animal communication is acute and to the point. You do not doubt yourself, but sometimes the resultsare hazy. This will become clear in time. You connect to the universe, the Oneness, and you are to come to us, your healing team everyday."

GERTIE (a friend's peahen)—You are sharp, clever, always seeking the. Your path with aches and triumphs is nil without the knowing of love, trust, and being in the light of the Universal Oneness."

MOLLY (my white Arabian mare)—"I am a part of your healing team and we all help you in anyway we can but especially in developing your clarity and sure-footedness as you learn to trust your communications with the animals. Continue your learnings in this area and talk to me all the time, everyday, as we share the blessed love of the All."

SPIRIT KITTY (my tabby cat)—
"Listen. I love you eternally. I can talk with you anytime but I need the atmosphere to be cleansed of negativity, cleared of kerfuffle, for us to be energetically in sync. Stand up tall and straight. Trust yourself. Be one with me. Mon ami, all is well. Play the game, win. You are up to this goal of becoming the animal healer you wish to manifest. I am here everyday for you. We are one.

Stop holding back. Move! Punch it, Bertha.

I was there for you, I came out of the woods three times, appeared out of nowhere, when your Mum went into the nursing home, when she died, when your house totally burned. I was there to comfort you. Don't you recognize me. I am your reincarnated Molly kitty, another beautiful tabby. You recognize now my life source, my higher soul, my embodiment of the All. It is the least I could do to be near you, see and touch and feel you, as you grieved. I remain now to help with your growing into animal healing and communication at the highest level."

SHEP (my border collie)—"I bring you these words of love and devotion as I prepare to cross over soon. Listen to the leaves. Hear their rustle, their rhythm, their never-ending love and living. Listen to the grass loving your feet on it, joyous to be green living. Listen to the wind. So happy to be caressing your face, waking you to possibilities, keeping you active and happy.

Listen to the water. Gurgling, gleeful, moving, transforming, shapeless, making waves and furrows and ripples, forever and by ever, lasting and being.

You are one with them all—Mitakuye oyasin."

SPAMMY (my German Shepard)—In meditation, I thanked him

I see in you the love and angelic awareness of Strongheart. You crossed over so early and I miss you but I am so happy I got to have you at my side for just a little while.

"I was Strongheart reincarnated. I am sorry I could not stay longer with you. I had many things to do. I am part of your team and I am here for you always. I am not with you necessarily to help you with healing the animals. Rather, I am of your higher self, your soul's journey, your development, your humility and strength. I am around you, surrounding you with love and strength, to aid you in growing into your highest being. In these ways I do help you with healing and psychic abilities."

LIBBY (my Haflinger mare)—
"I am not part of your direct healing team but I stand behind you at every reading. All of us, any of us, we all help you, love you, surround you in every way with light and understanding and knowledge. LIVE JOYOUSLY, laugh, be happy. All is well. All is as it should be."

So it is hoped and intentioned that any person reading these words will seek out the sacred and loving spirits of their own animals. Listen to their messages. Ask for their help. Be gracious to them. They want only the highest good for each of you.

CHAPTER 7

TRUST AND LOSS
A Lesson of Experiencing Animal Mysticism Through the Loss of a Beloved Pet

Any new relationship must begin with trust. There may be instant recognition on one side or perhaps both sides. It may take ages sometimes for one of the parties to finally develop absolute trust in the other. But trust there must be.

Trust arrives with a softening of the body, a relaxation in the eyes, an emanation of joy in the actions. It is that knowing of what is just and right can be found in the other. Trust is, then, love, pure love, of the highest order. It is what we all seek in the other. It is not an ephemeral experience but is strong, resilient, solid, a stone monument to all past sharing. The soul-being of an animal does not look for possibilities of non-trust. Nor should we. Trust is firm, beautiful, unwavering, even in the face of others bringing judgement, cruel harm, negativity, or unacceptance. Trust, firmly existing in the Universal All, comes in when it is with the highest energies of truth, wellness, and intent always of the the greatest good for all.

Thus, the trust relationship's destiny can only be of eternity, of love in all planes, all times, all dimensions. It is created and sustained by the sepharic energies of all animals with ease and knowing. Humans, on the other hand, have much to learn in their life lessons about what trust means and how it can be sustained. A person must create and intend trust to the point where it cannot be shaken by non-positive, low level vibrations or by nay-sayers, sadness, worry, disappointment, or anger. A human must bring their higher soul to fulfill and embrace this lesson of learning trust. It can only wither when you bring down your energy to diminishing pressures of fear, hurt, sickness, distrust, revenge, greed, selfishness, or ego-driven desires.

Learning to trust in trust is a billowing of the beautiful fulfillment of grace, absolute acceptance, non-judgmental love. Animal companions, as well as any animal encounters, allow that unfolding. Since the beginning of the everything, animals have brought us this gift. Why would anything but love sustain trust? There is nothing stronger, more stalwart, than love and the love of trusting. Living in the trust of the moment is impossible without the surrounding truest love, the pure clarity of existence, which brings the freeing of a soul, a blossoming of the forever of being.

Being one with animals is to learn the trust that, spiritually, animals are always moving through the non-positive parts of us and going right to our hearts. They allow us to how pure unconditional love can raise our spirits, bring us into the moment. Their lesson of trust brings us into a higher plane, a greater vibrational frequency, in which our own souls can expand and listen and create and bring to others that very essence of joy and rightness and protection our animals teach us. To bring us into the moment is to bring us into the presence of the Divine

Spirit. Animals as angelic beings always bring a connecting to the Great Unknown

Experiencing, therefore, the exiting of a beloved companion pet is difficult and emotionally draining, suddenly and devastatingly sad. There is a leaving, a loss of warmth and nurturing companionship, a raising of grief. How then can a person bring their devotion to their pet and continue relying on that bond of trust they shared in the physical, trusting that their forever-solid relationship of love remains in the spiritual?

An animal chooses to depart from its guardian, often in ways seemingly mysterious and unknown, and it is difficult in grief to trust that all is as it was planned. But the truth is, the soul of the guardian and the soul of the animal created their life paths while still in the spiritual plane, incorporating all those shared lessons and growths of experiences they chose, one of which was the death and crossing over back to home, to the realm of the Divine Sprit.

Being of and in "the flesh" does not define beings. No soul leaves to become nothing. Every soul is a loving vibrating unique energy that is always present, in all planes and dimensions and all times, ever in love and support, guiding from the spiritual side just as that spirit also manifested in the physical plane.

And so it is that experiencing the loss of a beloved companion pet is often a difficult lesson in trust. Trusting through the loss of a pet is to know that all is as it should be. Every soul is a loving vibrating unique energy that is always present, in all planes and dimensions and all times, ever in love and grace. Your pets in spirit are with you constantly. Thus, if you trust in the beautiful spirit of your animals, you will never doubt that from the "other side" your companions are surrounding you, bathing you in the white light of the All. You are never alone, never without them.

Be grateful for the time shared, remember the funny joyous moments and rejoice in the lessons learned together and the forever bonds of your two spirits. Absorb the magnanimous gift of love created by your beloved animal come from the angelic realm. And most importantly, bring that sunshine of becoming one with your pet in total acceptance and love on earth into an understanding of the shortness of the path chosen, the experience of passion and caring and total devotions and even deep grieving and healing. All evolved into one and the act of departure by your pet from the physical into the spiritual, the crossing over the rainbow bridge, was as planned and needed, fully joyful and fulfilled. A crossed-over pet instantly becomes closer to your heart spirit, and you will forever be listening to that divine input from your beloved pet.

Every animal dies. Every animal has a very quick transition, instantaneous, at death. For an animal, crossing over from the physical body to the spiritual existence is a seamless happening. There is nothing to hold them back, to keep them pinned in mortality, no ego or resistance. They return their flesh to Earth Mother and bring their spirit energy to become part of the collective whole of the Universal Spirit. Your pet exists as a whole unique individual in spirit as ever it was in the physical body, but now can be in limitless places at once, in toto without diminution of that energy. Its unique sacred being exists in all places and dimensions in all times. The pet just comes through and is instantly welcomed back into the higher realm and told, "Good job, well done, for the benefit of the whole." An animal can be communicated with immediately at death. There is no waiting. They are at once in the spiritual and whole again, angelic in their being.

Pet guardians often ask how it is that innocent pets leave us, especially when at very young ages. How is that karma? It is not karma. The animal was in service to the guardian for a pre-chosen amount of time and their dying has nothing to do with what the pet has done, e.g., karma. This is a contractual thing, arrived at in spirit, a divine contract of pet with guardian that creates chosen experiences in the physical life. The animal says: "I am going to be your pet, your animal son or daughter, but I am going to leave you within a few years or even shortly after birth. Because this is how you will learn to be more compassionate, be more patient, be more understanding, to truly grasp the feelings of grief and loss. This will be a sacred teaching and you will grow as a result."

So, in fact, your pet is doing an angelic deed by leaving. But that does not mean at a mortal level that it is any easier to deal with. Just knowing that doesn't help you as a guardian who has lost a pet. The grief is often huge and insurmountable, lingering for years sometimes.

The angelic souls of animals dying have no anger or fear or feelings of remorse or blame for humans. In psychic readings with them, they always ask their beloved guardians to release all emotions of guilt or sadness about the way the guardian acted when they were dying. Their love is always with the message of absolute non-judgmental love for their Mum and Dad.

Animals that have passed remain around their family of humans and other animals to make their love and caring from the other side known to their loved ones. They work at alleviating those feelings of grief, sadness and loneliness over their dying. No matter how many years go by, their Mums and Dads will feel or see or hear them. They offer protection, often nudging guardians to see to an undiagnosed illness coming up, or simply relieving anxiety of everyday turmoil.

When there is a death of a pet at any age around us, we tend to focus on what we are losing, what we are missing about our animals, and we understand that at a technical, spiritual, theoretical level that's not the point. We should focus on what they gave, what they brought to the table, what we value about them, what lessons we learned from them. But still, we go into that saying, "Ah, but I really miss them...I really don't have anybody to talk to now."

Learn from the animals. Your pet does not miss you or grieve after they cross over because they actually are here with you. Their spirit vibration of love and protection completely surrounds you and there is no sense of being separated from you. To them, things are ever as they were when in the physical.

So it is a hard wrestling match of emotions and true spiritual love. But the thing to really focus on is what they gave, the amount of love that was there. This is what they leave behind when they go. That's it. It becomes our job then to give away the love they shared with us. Know that your love shared is never lost, never diminished, but continues on forever. And in that realization, take what they gave you, walk with it, and give it to others. That's what is absolutely critical in understanding the sacredness of the love. It is the totality of the mysticism that your own beloved pet brought to you.

Here are messages from my readings with pets describing their own crossing over and love to their guardian Mums and Dads.

BABE

In the first example, we find Babe, a tiny elderly chihuahua, just shortly after she crossed over the rainbow bridge.

BABE'S MESSAGE
2016

Babe, may I speak with you at this time.

Babe. "Sure, Ma."

Can you tell me about your spirit, your higher self?

BABE. "Well, I am light (her image flashes) in the sense that I light the way, lead down the path, help to initiate the forward movement, the progress."

Is that why you were with your Mum in this lifetime?

BABE. "Oh yes—she needed to move forward to be in her place and her path. She had much to deal with, to conquer, and I was there with my energy, propelling her forward. We were quite close you know. We've had other lifetimes together, but this time was really special for us both. The bonding was so close we were almost one. She knows. She has seen herself grow, especially since my passing. My death was a milestone for her, a changing point, a marker. She got stronger in herself and in her plans for her life. She came of age, so to speak. I am still with her everyday. She knows. She has seen my glow in the hallway. She has told you also there is a special glow over my gravesite that brightens when she remembers me. All will be well. We will be together on this side soon with all my little brothers and sisters. Goldie (my own rescued golden retriever) is here. She says 'Hi—and thanks for taking care of her.'"

Is there anything else you want me to know?

BABE. "Not at this time. Many Blessings."

Thank you for speaking with me. And many blessings to you also.

CHANCE

Chance, a 9 year old male King Charles Cavalier, crossed over in an unexpected freak accident just the day before this reading with him. Understandably, his guardian was devastated at this sudden loss of her pet and she wanted him to know she was sorry. In this message, he brings strong images of shared past lives to better ease his Mum's sorrow.

CHANCE'S MESSAGE
October 11, 2021

Chance, may I do this reading with you?

CHANCE. "Sure, Ma."

Beginning the session, I lit a candle to carry my prayers for him in the smoke upward to Creator. I asked him to come forward to me in the tunnel of light between our hearts. He showed himself prancing and dancing, so lightly able to "jump and laugh," he says to me. He sits down in front of me, suddenly quite serious, staring at me.

CHANCE'S MESSAGE
October 11, 2021

Here is what Chance had to say—

CHANCE. "I know my Mum is grieving at my passing yesterday. Of course, I understand her sorrow and heaviness. There is no reason to take on this heavy burden. My love and absolute devotion to her will not allow her to view my crossing in this way. Please tell her all is as it should be and exactly as we planned it.

My Mum and I made a soul contract before reincarnating this time and in that plan we chose to share a lifetime together, however short in hours and days that might be. Our bonding and love is quite strong and we have shared many lifetimes before. I would not allow her another caring of a slowly dying being in this lifetime. She has sacrificed many times before and given her devotion to those in need who were dying."

I am shown two visions of Chance's Mum. The first is in a WWI tent with dying injured soldiers. She is wearing a Red Cross nurse's uniform as she moves from bed to bed, always taking each man's hand into hers and talking quietly and lovingly, knowing in her heart he would soon be dying from his wounds. Her grief is absorbed and set aside as she puts each patient first in her thoughts and ministrations.

Next I am shown her sitting in a high-backed wicker chair wearing a longish dress with a cat on her lap. The cat is terminally ill and her every stroke on his fur is to comfort and warm him as he begins to pass over. Her words to him are of gratitude for being her very special kitty and how happy she was to have had him, even if only for a short time. She was even then in a higher vibration of knowing that life in the physical is time to give love, to learn new lessons on loss and regeneration.

Chance now speaking says to his Mum: "I want you to know that I was with you, by your side, in both of these scenes and many many more as you and I have shared many lifetimes in the past. I send you this message of reaching into your higher spiritual self and bringing understanding of our sacred pact together. This was a shared happiness and laughter and closeness of two beings, you and I. It was my choice this lifetime to die quickly and in good health. I chose not to go through again the agonies of old age and feeling of helplessness in being in a sickly dying body. I know you honor that was my

choice. But again, I emphasize that I wanted you spared this lifetime of grieving over me as an elderly, senile, crippled Chance. And that you agreed to this.

I want you to know I feel your grieving but my every energetic vibration to you today is this—remember me and cherish me as a happy, young, vibrant, loving and lovable buddy-boy, always at your side. If you need a memory, let it be with a candle lit and prayerful thanks to me for all the shared times. I am forever grateful to you.

You are growing into your spirituality in a great way in this lifetime. I will be guiding you and opening doors for you to continue in this path, which I can accomplish so easily from the other side, the spiritual realm." (And he is showing me another dog and 2 cats beside him, a team of heavy hitters working together for your greatest good.) "You could not have a more loving and devoted coterie of friends cheering you on as you continue to grow in love and understanding and intuitive work helping others. They are all so very proud of your accomplishments." (I was shown them all doing fist-pumps (paw-pumps) in the air as they are saying, "Yay, hurrah, and good for you.")

"Lastly, know that yesterday, my crossing over day, was chosen as a significant date—or set of numbers…10-10." (Chance was telling his Mum to watch for those numbers to appear in the future for a significant reason.) "We can now best transmit knowings to you as you sleep. We ask that you to keep a bedside diary for recording these dreams. Their significant lessons and learnings will deepen and grow into your life as you move forward."

Is there anything else, Chance?

CHANCE. "No, Ma. Go in peace."

And you also, Chance.

CYRUS

The third reading is from Cyrus, a 20 year old gray male horse, who was quite sick at the time. His guardian Mum was very upset that the vet visits did not seem to be healing him and she wanted to know if there was anything she could do to help him. In his message, Cyrus was strongly preparing his Mum for his crossing, bringing her to a better understanding of what that entails spiritually and lovingly for the two of them.

CYRUS'S MESSAGE
February 23, 2020

Cyrus, may I speak to you at this time?

CYRUS. "Sure, Ma."

Cyrus, how are you doing today?

CYRUS. "Not good, Ma. Yes, I am knowing who you are completely and sweetly in spirit and in< physical. Your Molly (my own elderly horse still in physical) stands beside me to help me balance and to warm my body. Just like two old, old white horses —of kin and kinship."

May I do an energy healing with you, Cyrus?

CYRUS. "Yes and no, Ma. I welcome your warm and comforting energy to ease my physical body but I do not wish for you to bring in the vibrating energies of grounding. The feeling I have and choose is one of freedom and lightness and you are aware and full of the light to not want that stolid energy of grounding, binding me to Mother Earth."

May I see your physical body and be shown what is causing you distress?

CYRUS. "Yes, Ma. My stomach lining will be shown to you as red and painful and my stomach is bloated, not working at all. My intestines will be shown to you as tangled and swollen in areas. The soreness and pain is very draining and,

Will the vet be able to help you, Cyrus?

CYRUS. "Perhaps, but it will happen all over again and I do not wish to feel this sick again. Can you tell my Mum?"

Yes, Cyrus. I will tell her. What can your Mum do to help you at this time?

CYRUS. "Well, Ma. Some painkiller medicine would be so nice and some great quiet. Some gentle stroking on my face and not leaving me alone all night would be so comforting. Please tell my Mum, of course I know she loves me. Would that be ever so? Of course. Would my love for her be ever more? Of course.

My Mum and I have shared many things—fun and wind and joy and racing fast and laughing into the sun. We have shared tears and hard times too. I have taught her many lessons—MANY lessons —and she has been a good student/learner. There is yet one great lesson I wish to give her that is so important for her spirit to grow and blossom. It is the lesson of 'letting go.' This does not mean forgetting or disrespecting or loss of love or loss of warmth and communal vibrating energies when a loved one moves into the spiritual plane. It does mean acknowledging that all is one, that is, that I exist both in the physical plane and in the soul plane, both and one at the same time. When I cross over, I want my Mum to embrace the new me in the spiritual, be so very happy for a pain-free being, happy that I am able to continue my work on the other side and to add to that with many spiritual lessons for those still in the physical that I was unable to do while still on earth. And so it is with all my Mum's beings now in spirit.

Yes, my Mum will grieve my passing and my not being with her in flesh and blood in a big warm loving gray body of a horse. But I will be SO with her in spirit. She will hear and feel the energy of a loud neigh, the plop clop of my hooves as I am near her, always in spirit. It is a big lesson, letting go, but it opens so many higher, beautiful, loving and healing pathways and allows for the helping and healing of so many needed little ones here with my Mum. I will be her mentor in each and every healing she learns to do with being a conduit of the energy of the All. Her humility and acceptance of this new life path, I will help her know and grow. Please let her know all of this—and keep strong in her memory—so that her path forward is easy, smooth, lovely and loving, giving, and calm. I will embrace her in each moment."

Anything else, Cyrus?

CYRUS. "No, Ma. Go in peace."

And you also, Cyrus

GUNTHER

And lastly, a message from a sweet older Miniature Wire-Haired Dachshund named Gunther who had terminal heart problems and wanted to give his Mum a message.

GUNTHER'S MESSAGE
September 17, 2016

Gunther, may I speak with you?

GUNTHER. "Yes, Ma. I am dying and my Mum is upset about that."

I understand, Gunther. Are you still walking?
GUNTHER. "Oh yes, just a little slower. My heart is slowing. My Mum is upset at this time. She needs to know that I am with her and will be on the other side also. We will have the same conversations, our same walk-abouts, our same exchanges of love and light. I am in her and she, with me. We are one together, pure love. Tell her to rock back and find a spot on her lap for me to cuddle. She will know I am there. The little guy (his younger doggie brother) needs lots of love. He won't know what to do when I am gone, Tell my Mum to love him and cradle him and rock him after I am gone."

Thank you, Gunther.

GUNTHER. "My pleasure."

By reading these messages from pets who had crossed over or were about to leave to the spiritual plane, it is hoped a new understanding will come of the loving bonds of animals and their guardians which brings trust in the strength of never-ending love and an uplifting feeling of joy.

CHAPTER 8

GROWING OLD —
Eternal Love, Lingering Memories, Stories of Forever Bonds

The life-long sharing with a beloved animal can best be summed up as a billet doux, an eternal spiritual bond. There is no coming and going or fading of shared times. The immensity and beauty of it simply morphs into angelic knowingness, a trust of one in the other, that transits all time, all space, all dimensions. It is forever.

On a cold January day in 2020, I had to make the difficult decision to have my great white horse, Molly, and my small brown Shetland pony, Roxie, euthanized because of old age and illness. I had tied prayer ties of tobacco into their manes and went out to say goodbye to both of them several times, offering carrots and apples.

As I was meditating awaiting the arrival of the vet, a surge of warm energy entered my chest and I saw before me my life guide, Chief Sitting Bull, a great Lakota chief. He was not as usual sitting astride his own faithful white horse but stood with arms crossed and wearing his full eagle headdress. He told me that this time he was standing because he was waiting to ride my white horse across to the spiritual plain of rolling hills and tall grass and showed me riding on the wind atop Molly with faithful little Roxie trotting right along side them.

He said I was to honor the Lakota ancestors by being a brave and strong Lakota woman, showing me with facial paint marks and a headband with two beautiful feathers in it. I knew we were all preparing for this day and Molly and Roxie projected understanding of the circle of life, knowing not only would they be met on the other side by their tiospaye (family) but would be someday on the reception end when I crossed over. At that moment, I was not alone but was surrounded in a circle by a wolf, a bear, and other animals including my own cats and dogs sitting together to my right. I was not alone in this incredibly sad and traumatic moment but in loving hands.

Later, a Lakota crossing-over ceremony with heated Grandfather Stones, prayers, sacred tobacco, and songs was done in remembrance of the return of the spirits of Molly and Roxie to the Star Nation and the Ancestors.

Growing Old

Look into this flame of fire during the ceremony and see my beloved white horse in a sudden bright flash leaping upward, a sign to me of her return to spirit, letting me know she was present and ever with me.

Her words of comfort came in a message shortly after, describing our many years together as a threesome with our sweet Roxie. Her consolation and assurance of our forever togetherness gave healing of my grief and a warmed heart of gratefulness.

Donna
Dry your eyes
There is no reason to cry
all is as it was meant to be
i lived exactly as i was
our friendship strong and lasting
is now in spirit and ever present
we have no regrets
by we i mean we three
lived in perfect timing
a heaven on earth for we two
at the hands of your diligence
yes diligence at our care
i look forward with gratitude to the future
painless for us now
only in joy
we are at your side
in your house
in the ether
and forever in the pasture
close your eyes and see us there
feel our presence
our enduring friendship is
ever present and ever lasting
you may draw on it's strength as your own
for today and for always
we are bound together
by choice
and by choice we lived
and continue to do
ever present
by your side

With love and gratitude, depths of which are
not able to be properly expressed,
Molly
your friend in spirit

Here then are readings for two beloved dogs who crossed over more than 60 years ago and for whom their guardian still grieved:

PAL AND SHAFFER

My dear friend now in her 80's asked that a reading be done with her two beloved dogs, Pal and Schaffer. Pal was a male black lab who from a puppy was her constant companion growing up and into her teen years. When Ruth went off to college, tragically her mother soon after had the dog euthanized because she did not want the responsibility of taking care of him. My friend, 60 years on, still grieved for him and carried feelings of anger and sorrow and guilt that she could not have protected him. Here is his message to his beloved friend.

PAL'S MESSAGE
July 16, 2018

Hi Pal. May I communicate with you?

Pal. "Yes, Ma."

How are you doing?

Pal. "Just great. Love it here—peaceful and serene and full of love."

Tell me about the essence of you.

Pal. "I am not light but splendor, not dark but white, not apples but plum, cherry, and pear, not heavy feet and dragging but bouncy, bouncy, dancing. I am so full of joy I could burst."

Can you tell me about your life on this plane with Ruth?

Pal. "Oh yes—we were close pals, sympatico. She knew my thoughts and I knew hers."

I see a yellow ball. Is that yours?

Pal. "No, it was Ruth's but she let me play with it sometimes. We had so much fun, rolling, wrestling in the grass, listening to leaves blowing along the ground, watching blue sky, and "communing" so to speak. She brought me the best food, the very best food. And she talked to me— a lot."

I see him howling. Why do I see you howling?

Pal. "I howled when she left me—so alone, so alone. Where was she?"

Do you understand now where she was?

Pal. "Yes, of course. Her divine pathway was set and she had to leave. All happened as planned."

What was your divine mission when you were living with Ruth?

Pal. "My main task was to lighten her life, bring her joy which she was badly needing, to lift her spirit to the highest level of love so she would know what was possible. She needed me in her life—a stability, a knowing of solidness, an easement of growing into adulthood. I watch over her, you know. Always have, always will. Tell her I am there— if she sees a black shadow flitting across, that is me. I bring her quietness and acceptance now and always."

How old were you when you passed?

Pal. "About 5."

Can you describe your passing?

Pal. "Fear, then floating, then utter, utter joy. I flew to Ruth just then—put my paws on her shoulders, looked into her eyes, and wrapped her in love. I knew her grief. I knew her anger. But all is forgiven, all here is love and forgiveness. It can be no other way.

Tell Ruth her grief was received here and although she was inconsolable for a while, always, always she was being sent the white light of love to surround her and quiet her. In her heart she knows this is so. She often saw the white column of light, whether a stream of sunshine or in her dreams. I sent that to her so she could move on, make her plans with determination and grit and pluck and ABSOLUTE integrity and love. And good for her! She succeeded. Tell her she is loved every day. I send my love as do all her guidance and the angels."

Was that you holding your paw up yesterday as I was thinking of our session?

Pal. "Naw—that was Schaffer. He's such a clown—always was, always will be. He's waiting to be next to talk to you."

Is there anything else you want to communicate to Ruth?

Pal. "Just tell her I am here and will be there when she passes, 'paw-in-hand,' so to speak. We have some plans to talk over. All is good. All is love and patience and fulfillment.

Thank you for talking with me.

Pal. "My pleasure."

SCHAFFER (Busy-doer in German)

Schaffer was a male black lab who was about 5 years old when he crossed over. He lived with Ruth in the southwest where she was teaching. When she reached down to turn off the alarm clock in the morning, he copied her motion with his head bowing to it. She laughed at this but felt bad then for making fun of him. She left him with people living in her house while she made a trip to Germany but they treated him badly and tied him to a tree. He only lived about 1 1/2 yrs. after her return. She feels guilty for leaving him and perhaps precipitating his early death.

SCHAFFER'S MESSAGE
July 16, 2018

Do I have permission to speak to you, Schaffer?

Schaffer. "Yes, Ma."

Hi Schaffer. How are you doing?

Schaffer. "Just great, you know. It's a great pleasure to finally talk to you. I have been waiting."

So you knew your Mum would ask for a session for you?

Shaffer. "Oh yea—of course. Lot's happening, things to get done/accomplished. She needed to speak to me and, "Voila!" It's all arranged. I am here for you."

Is there a way you would like to communicate to me/to your Mum?

Shaffer. "Sure. I'll do the talking and you listen."

Okay—I've got it. I understand. I am ready.

Shaffer. "So here goes. Tell the gal I am here, so alive, so full of it. Energy, energy plus. Bouncing with joy to finally talk to her. Tell her we had such a GOOD life together. Wasn't it fun? I tried to make you laugh—in so many ways. Like the alarm clock set-up you told Donna about. That was meant for you to laugh—not chuckle. Laugh out loud! Great way to start the day! Surely you saw me grinning ear-to-ear, so to speak. Why would you feel guilty for laughing at me. It was fun, sheer, pure fun. Wow—what a life we had. Togetherness, trips, rides, eating, talking, sharing. Yeah—you talked to me, babe, and I talked right back. You understood most of it, too.

When you left, I was sad. Of course, I was sad. But my divine mission with you also had to include teaching to the people you left me with. Their lives needed to witness abandonment, lack of caring. Their higher souls were attuning to these things and their paths were altered by the experience with me. Do not fret, little one. My divine mission with you was also to expose these same things to you through those people. You needed that experience to help you on your path.

I loved you your entire life. I was with you in spirit long before we actually lived together. And I am still with you, as if I had never left your side."

I see a porch with lattice wood on the side. What does this mean?

Shaffer. "It is a place, a place we shared. Summer fun. Tell her about the back, the fun, the lounging. We had fun—solace—joy—sharing. It was all good, even the bad."

Why did you have your paw up when I saw you before the session?

Shaffer. "Just a sign for Ruth. She will know it is me, for sure. Nothing ends, all is forever. Our shared love is forever and it brought joy to the universe. I'll be here waiting when you cross, Ruth. But I am with you all the time, breathing down your neck. Standing on your bed— oh yeah! Those indents are my paw prints. So don't fret, don't mourn. All is well—and just as it should be. Love you always."

Thank you for talking with me, Schaffer.

Shaffer. You bet. Tell her to talk to me! I am there.

RUTH'S RESPONSE TO THE READINGS WITH PAL AND SCHAFFER

"Thanks so much, Donna. These are both messages I want to read over many times. I now realize I had perfect companionship with all the dogs and cats I've had through the years. These messages have made me feel happy and content—both for their well-being and joy, their knowing how much I loved them and grieved for their passing, and for their constant love for me.

Pal really did bring me joy and love in a way I hadn't ever experienced at 13 or so to almost 18. We did play ball and tumble and run and bike and commune. And Schaffer was so perfect for me too. He just appeared and we were so in tune with each other. The porch you saw was my back porch there with a kind of roof and a lattice on the side.

I will spend some time talking with Pal and Schaffer. You have opened up an avenue of communication for me that I hadn't realized was there."

Lastly, as I continue to miss my big white sweet mare, Molly, and my little roly-poly pony, Roxie, I return often to read once more Molly's words to me after their passing together several years ago.

Growing old is made easier, softer, more kind, more bearable in the physical, when it is shared with your animal companion. And the same is just as true for your aging animal. As Ram Dass wrote about caregiving, "We are all just walking one another home."

This leaning on one another comes so easily in the soft furry body of an animal which relishes old shaky hands stroking and caressing, those hands so needing to feel the warm peace of the pet on their lap. And likewise, an arthritic hip in elderly pet is soothed and warmed by human hand. Neither partner sees aging infirmities in the other nor makes judgement of frailty and forgetfulness. If two become one, then neither need worry about acceptance and caring flowing into the coming crossing-over. Love is indeed forever, an eternal truth.

Conquering Animal Mysticism

CHAPTER 9
THE LITTLE ONES

Fearing, despising, disliking or having phobias of the "little ones" brings you into a lower consciousness. Do you feel repulsed in an encounter with a spider, an ant, a snake, a mouse, a mosquito, a bat? Are these "little ones" so much different from a pet guinea pig, a butterfly, a robin?

We fear what we do not know. We dismiss the living soul of anything we deem is not a beauty of God's creation. We know nothing of that ugly "little one's" part in the scheme of the world, in the tapestry that interweaves to keep us all alive. We do not feel gratitude and joy for the existence of this "little one." In fact, we know nothing of the golden energy, the loving positive gift from Creator.

For people who find the "little ones" repulsive, it is dispiriting and soul searing to go on that way.   If we would seek a new consciousness, a higher being-ness of soul, then know we can search in all things for beauty, humor and future promise. If we will but acknowledge the higher level of communication with all things, we will recognize the need to be kind in our thoughts and emotions, carrying only positive images of all animals. Know we are one— spiritually even to the vibrating energies of DNA shared, the same but for a very few different genes and expressions.

Realize that spirit and soul are the only permanent truths that matter. It is best to let go, allow and surrender, give Creator the trust and love that will allow us to respect, love without judgement, accept without rejection, all these "little ones." Embrace them as our own, protect them, give them dignity and allow that their purpose in existing is just as ours, no less and no more. The frequency vibration of every creature is unique and cannot be compared to any other. Be humble and be grateful for each creature, fluffy and cute or scaly-skinned and not so cute, and thank them for their work they do in the light and love of the All. Their existence is as important to the universe as is your own.

HERCULES

Here now are beautiful messages from a spider who came unexpectedly and unsummoned into a reading I was doing for a sick dog named Percy and his Mum, Lenna. Find delight and uplift from his words.

This small black hoppy (jumping) spider has shown up on my keyboard just now. I have gently put him outside. Well, he did hop off the paper on which I was carrying him which was a long fall and hope he is OK. I couldn't find him on the ground.
He did stop and sat back on rear legs before being placed on the paper and stared at me. I am asking now for the message brought forward by him.

HERCULES' MESSAGE
FEBRUARY 26, 2021

"I am Hercules, better known as Herc to my friends. I bring you greetings this rainy cool day. Our paths will probably not cross again but the message I bring you is of the utmost and highest order. You are to continue in your healing work. We know, all of us in the spider clan, how you honor each day by your prayer that all the little ones who are feared or despised or dismissed because of their appearance, or role in Mother Earth's survival, be cared for and we know that you are sending loving energy for their very beings.

Now here is your message for Percy and Lenna from us. We see the struggle for life to continue and for the difficult days of breathing and slowed energy for Percy and for her Mum's distress at this. We bring Creator's promise that all is being shared—the caring and the warm love and the angst and sadness. You are not alone. The bright white light of Creator is seen around you and amplified by the angels and guides of both Percy and Lenna.

We, the spider clan, wish for you to acknowledge this protection and support and positive outlook and joy from all the spirits surrounding you. By acknowledging this, you will be strong in your heart and body and be able to cope with your angst and sadness. If you cannot actually feel and see these loving spirits around you, Lenna, know that every time from now on that you encounter one of us, we are bringing you that reminder of the spirit love surrounding you and 'to keep the faith, baby.' Percy, of course, knows each of us in the spider clan and always thanks us for all the good and loving ones who support her at this time."

Percy now shows himself putting a tiny gold crown on the head of each spider in a semicircle around him, thanking them for their help.

HERCULES. "Thank you, Ma, for allowing us to share this message with Lenna and Percy. In all good things in the forever, your friend, Herc."

Thank you, Herc. I am so very glad to have your gifts of message and hope. I honor you for your very being.

Later, as I continued to see tiny spiders near me, sometimes dangling of a tiny thread in front of my face, I inquired if there was more to learn from my little friends. This is the message given to me:

THE SPIDER CLAN AND HERCULES

FEBRUARY 28, 2021

"We are here to bring your attention to the smallest things. You are one of us but your form in physical is large. We bring you great comfort and caring—more than you can even imagine from our small bodies.

I hung in front of your eyes. I healed you. I slowed your heart, relaxed your body, removed your anxiety. of having your cataract surgeries. I came to remind you—pay attention to the tiniest energies. They are your guides at this time.

I glint in the sun with the strength and care and sudden bright light you receive. I pave your way in writing and healing the animals.

We bring you positiveness—believe this strongly. You will be okay. Be creative. Be strengthened. Watch for us in everything you do. We will bring you warmth, care, and soothing. We send out our love from the here and from the other side. Aho!"

LILO

Milo is a female yellow-bellied slider turtle who has been with her guardian, Alicia, for the two years since she was a tiny new hatchling. She is now about adult size and lives within a large aquarium of water with a resting place above water. Alicia speaks with her often and interacts with Lilo outside the aquarium.

Alicia feels a strong bond with Lilo, more so than with any other pets she has had. In this communication ready, Alicia wanted to find out if Lilo was happy, how she might converse better with Lilo, and what type of food she would like to have.

Immediately on beginning this reading, I was shown visiting energies of Lilo. She was being supported and encouraged by the many eons of the turtle clan which have gone before her. I was told she chose this life form in order to be with and bind closely with her guardian. I felt a huge, mighty energy being brought to her so that she may help her beloved Alicia grow into her full spiritual self. There was no happenstance in Lilo making her way into Alicia's space, her physical being. This was a divine plan, contract if you like, between the two of them before returning to earth. It was a creating of shared paths in which they both will many experiences which will illuminate the grace and and love of the Divine Source to many around them. Alicia and Lilo have been together in many previous lifetimes. Most recently, Lilo was a cat—thin, lithe, long upright tail, very strong in spirit.

LILO'S MESSAGE
July 23, 2021

Lilo, may I do this reading with you?

LILO. "Sure, Ma. It is a great honor to greet one of the ancients such as myself. I know and interact with your crocodile clan at many levels, we of the ancient times and ancient knowledge, keepers of the records and communications. So welcome, dear one. It is good to talk with you. It is important for my Mum to be helped to understand my 'being' and our bonding—or shall I call it our 'masterminding' — for that is what we are doing. We are co-creating an important path, a shared path, for elevating awareness and giving loving blessings to the human beings. The air is changing, the weather and sun and earth and fire are all bringing movement towards higher vibrational positive energies—wherein the spirits/souls can all move out and up and into their highest potentials. My Mum will have a strong role in this. She already feels the pull of the earth and the earth creatures who will help her grow into her higher spiritual self. We will speak more of these shortly."

Thank you for your greeting, Lilo. I am honored to be with you. I invited her own guides and angels to help with this reading and many turtles, all sizes, shapes, and colors, appeared in a semicircle around her. I was told these represented the many eons of the turtle clan which have gone before her.

LILO'S MESSAGE
July 23, 2021

"To continue the above words, I exist now in this space and time with my Mum to share our great love once again on the physical place. Yes, indeed she feels a strong love for me, an energy which swirls back and forth between us. It makes her happy and light to receive my positive vibrational energy and I too am elated and protected by her loving energy sent to me. Please tell her that NO thought or kind deed or laughing, loving sharing is lost on me. She feels this extraordinary lifting of vibrations and it brings my Mum into a level and space of being that is so very important to her growth and blossoming. There is much for her to grow into and her psychic intuition will expand as she invites me to aid her in this.

Please ask my Mum to take time each day, even if only for a few minutes, to close her eyes, take a deep breath, and allow the healing and love of the All in come into her. She can hold me in her hands and ask the same for me—as I also request each and every day for her.

The Turtle Clan magnetism is great and surrounds my Mum. It is filled with communication abilities and keeping of the ancient knowledge. It is hers to use as soon as she chooses. Together, we have much to accomplish, what the humans are now calling 'being light workers.' But that description falls short of the magnitude and magnificence of the power and love that drives, supports, moves forward toward the 'new earth' energy, balanced and thriving and protecting all things here. My Mum will grow into this step by step and be a truly giving and compassionate soul who will help so many, animals and humans and plants and earth and environment and all.

Please tell my Mum thank you for taking such good care of me. I am grateful for each and every thing she does for me, for always giving me love and great food and caring. It sustains me and keeps my health and happy self in good order. Dear Mum, we are on our way."

Anything else, Lilo?

"No, Ma. Go in peace."

And you also, Lilo.

In ending, please be so very aware that even the tiniest of living beings are sacred, carrying mysticism enlightenment for each human willing to listen and be imbued with their wisdom.

CHAPTER 10
Conquering Animal Mysticism— The Final Illumination

Animals are natural psychics and their abilities derive from their sacred and spiritual souls, beings with the highest of angelic vibrational energies. They as "light workers" guide, heal, and support human companions—and all living beings. As such, these divine messengers of mysticism come from the One Source in all their work.

Levels at which animals create these teaching and healing energy vibrations include:

- **Mental**—assisting with acuity and accuracy in human perceptions and communication.
- **Emotional**—helping the imbalance of people and the home surrounding, particularly by taking on unsettled emotional energies which may even result in their own physical behavior changes such as pacing and yowling.
- **Physical**—dealing with those imbalances (diseases of the body) in the guardians around them, animals

will try to cure or reduce these physical ailments, even to the extent quite often of taking on the energy imbalance into their own bodies, causing them to develop the exact same disease as their human parent such as diabetes, lymphoma, heart tumor, etc.

- **Spiritual**—urging people to clear and balance their higher spiritual energies, thereby bringing them into a "self- awakening." Within the spiritual sacredness, animals with their mysticism hold the memories of people's chosen life paths.

THEY REMEMBER

"His iridescence undiminished by death, I cradled the hummingbird gently in my hands. He had come a long way, this little warrior of light, and now his journey was over. I knew I must honor him. I could do no less for his time here, as fleeting as my own, was no less sacred. I placed him in a red silk shroud, tucking within it two blossoms to get him the rest of the way home. I then laid him to rest beneath the small temple in my garden that faces the rising sun. Within days a beautiful pink double blossomed calla lily sprouted. I have no other lilies in my garden. At the feeders on the patio, a small squadron of five hummingbirds gathered. I watched them and as though acknowledging my poor efforts for their lost one, they gathered together, rose up as one, hovered near me then flew away. I know this: We are all connected... the loss of one is a loss to all and honoring Life is a Sacred task."

LINDA BELLES
August 02, 2022

THEY HOLD THE BONDS OF LOVE

He was a cat. Long-haired, black, devoted to his guardian, Harriet, even as she struggled through cancers in her old age. Smokey Bear's sacrifice of living for her even into his own elderly, crippled, three-legged self is a story of deep of love and caring best told in his own words.

SMOKEY BEAR

June 6, 2019

"Today I am achy in my bones. The warmth of summer sunshine helps as does Harriet's hand on my back, hearing her talk to me and seeing her every day. I am fine, just doing my cat thing here in this life of freedom, rambling, eating.

The essence of me is this: I am soft, pattering rain, I am designs in the green leaves, I am sunlight and dripping drops off the trees. I am lightness, airiness, joy even though I have to hop on three legs. I am grinning and happiness. My voice is the voice of angels, bringing bells and cymbals and harps to this side for Harriet to enjoy.

My Mum, Harriet, and I were together in other lifetimes. She recognized me right away when I came to her. We have a healing bond of love—shared medicine, so to speak, in this lifetime. But we had other lives, rollicky good times, where we were there for each other. She knows when she looks in my eyes and sees flashes of other times and places with me.

My beloved Harriet is not to fret about me. I am fine and will stay as long as she needs me. My purpose in this lifetime was to share gratitude and love with her, to make her feel whole in body and spirit, so she could continue down her path. She is a tough cookie but nonetheless she needed me and I was there for her. I see the beautiful green leaves in the quilt she is making. I send thanks for taking care of me and sharing our beautiful life. She knows our sharing, our bond, is special. It is what we have created—so loving and warm and sustaining and nurturing of each other, ever even unto the spiritual realm."

TO END WITH

Animals are psychics and communicate in many intricate ways. There are, of course, the usual doggie ways—an eye blink, a snort, a yawning, a wag of the tail, a dip of the the head, a staring. But keep in mind that they are quite capable of mind-to-mind communication, both with you and among all the animals around them. This is a constant and ongoing exchange of energy and they are quite aware of your thoughts, your plans, your emotions, your anticipations. And they are aware of future events—even if you are not yet knowing them.

If you will but acknowledge this higher level of communication, you will recognize the need to be kind in your thoughts and emotions, carry only positive images of your pet, their health, their playtime, their behaviors. This is a great force for you to move in grace with your animals.

Know you are one. The animals, your pets, have an existence equally important to the universe as your own. Honor their work as the angelic beings they are and thank them daily, listing all the wonderful and delightful things they bring each day. As psychic beings yourselves, learn to mind-meld with your animals, and thus grow into your own spirituality and psychic abilities.

Everything discussed here with living animals is exactly the same for plants and any beings of the spiritual universe. You need only think of them and they are instantly with you. You can ask them your questions, express your heartache, enjoy and be refreshed by their beauty and caring. Respect the animals' intelligence and connect with that in love and joyful happiness. They are the one source of unconditional love we come to depend on. Thank them always with gratitude. You need only ask for their help, for they are eager and most lovingly willing.

Conquering Animal Mysticism

MITAKUYE OYASIN
WE ARE ALL ONE

References

Front cover
    photograph of horse, iStock by Getty Images

Title page
    photograph of pony by PixbyJenn.Zenfolio.com

Preface
    photograph of candles by Mike Labrum, unsplash.com

Introduction
    photograph of cat by Tina Marie Gancarz, Animal Communicator. tinamarieac.com

Chapter 1
    photograph of dog by PixbyJenn.Zenfolio.com

Chapter 2
    artwork by Heather Simmons
    photograph of conure by Amanda Root, psychic. snowmoontarot.com
    photograph of dog and guardian by Charlene Alverado

Chapter 3
    photograph of white dog by PixbyJenn.Zenfolio.com
    photograph of black dog by Tina Marie Gancarz (and communication scribed by Tina Marie Gancarz, Animal Communicator, tinamarieac.com)
    photograph of fish by Jennifer Rogers Mezydio (and communication scribed by Tina Marie Gancarz, Animal Communicator. tinamarieac.com)

Chapter 5
    photograph of cat by Alexsander Alves, unsplash.com poem by Linda Belles, psychic, LRBelles, psychic.
    LRBelles@comcast.net photograph of cat by Therese Bittner photograph of guide dog by Shuri S.

References

CHAPTER 6
    photograph of cat by Donna Sauer, Animal Communicator. dr.dlsauer@gmail.com
    referral to "Strongheart" in communication with dog, Spammy: Boone, J. Allen. 1954. Kingship with All Life. HarperCollins, NYC, NY
    photograph of horse by Doug Swinson, unsplash.com

CHAPTER 7
    photograph of white and gold dog by Heidi Mark photograph of black dog by Carolyn Thompson

CHAPTER 8
    photograph of fire by Tina Marie Gancarz, Animal Communicator. tinamarieac.com
    photograph of horse by Donna Sauer, Animal Communicator. dr.dlsauer@gmail.com
    poem scribed by Tina Marie Gancarz, animal communicator. tinamarieac.com
    quote by Ram Dass: Dass, Ram. Be Here Now. Lama Foundatio, San Christobal, NM.
    artwork by Heather Simmons

CHAPTER 9
    photograph of spider by Timothy Dykes, unsplash.com

CHAPTER 10
    photograph of pagoda by Margie Deck "They Remember," by Linda Belles, psychic. LRBelles@comcast.net
    photograph of cat by Donna Sauer, Animal Communicator. dr.dlsauer@gmail.com

BACK COVER
    photograph of pony by PixbyJenn.Zenfolio.com
    photograph of cat by Tina Marie Gancarz, animal communicator. tinamarieac.com

About the Author

Dr. Donna Sauer

Animal Energy Balancing and Healing

Animal Communication and Divine Purpose

Certified Animal Energy Intuitive
Lynn McKenzie Institute
Reiki Master
Lakota healing traditions
BSEd Biology, MS Zoology, PhD Biology

Her intuitive animal communication readings and energy healing sessions are coupled with writing and teachings of animal communication skills. At the heart of her work is the intention of helping each unique being come into their fullest life path with unconditional love.

Contact Information and to Schedule a Reading

Donna Sauer, PhD
Animal Intuitive and Energy Healer
dr.dlsauer@gmail.com

CPSIA information can be obtained
at www.ICGtesting.com
Printed in the USA
BVHW090235130123
656165BV00021B/899